Circle Time
Science

Written by Susan Finkel
and Karen Seb___

Illustrated by Gary Mo___

Teaching & Learning Company
1204 Buchanan St., P.O. Box 10
Carthage, IL 62321

This book belongs to

_____

Special thanks to Building Blocks Child Care Center in Burlington, Iowa, for all of their help with this cover photograph. We had a blast!

The activity portrayed on the front cover is described on page 33.

Cover by Gary Mohrman

Copyright © 1996, Teaching & Learning Company

ISBN No. 1-57310-065-X

Printing No. 98765432

Teaching & Learning Company
1204 Buchanan St., P.O. Box 10
Carthage, IL 62321-0010

Table of Contents

Be Kind to Your Web-Footed Friends . . .7
Observation
Prediction
Problem Solving
Communication

The Eency Weency Spider 15
Observation
Prediction
Problem Solving
Communication

Humpty Dumpty 19
Observation
Prediction
Problem Solving
Communication

I Went to the Animal Fair 25
Observation
Prediction
Problem Solving
Communication

Little Arabella Miller 31
Observation
Prediction
Problem Solving
Communication

Little Bo Peep 37
Observation
Prediction
Problem Solving
Communication

Little Jack Horner 42
Observation
Prediction
Problem Solving
Communication

London Bridge 46
Observation
Prediction
Problem Solving
Communication

Mister Sun 52
Observation
Prediction
Problem Solving
Communication

The North Wind Doth Blow 56
Observation
Prediction
Problem Solving
Communication

Open Them, Shut Them 63
Observation
Prediction
Problem Solving
Communication

Peanut Butter and Jelly 68
Observation
Prediction
Problem Solving
Communication

There Was a Little Turtle 74
Observation
Prediction
Problem Solving
Communication

Twinkle, Twinkle, Little Star 81
Observation
Prediction
Problem Solving
Communication

Two Little Apples 87
Observation
Prediction
Problem Solving
Communication

Where Is Thumbkin? 93
Observation
Prediction
Problem Solving
Communication

Every reasonable attempt has been made to identify copyrighted material.

Table of Science Processes

Observation

"Be Kind to Your Web-Footed Friends" 7
"The Eency Weency Spider" 15
"Humpty Dumpty" 19
"I Went to the Animal Fair" 25
"Little Arabella Miller" 31
"Little Bo Peep" .37
"Little Jack Horner" 42
"London Bridge" .46
"Mister Sun" 52
"The North Wind Doth Blow" 56
"Open Them, Shut Them" 63
"Peanut Butter and Jelly" 68
"There Was a Little Turtle 74
"Twinkle, Twinkle, Little Star" 81
"Two Little Apples" 87
"Where Is Thumbkin?" 93

Problem Solving

"Be Kind to Your Web-Footed Friends" 7
"The Eency Weency Spider" 15
"Humpty Dumpty" 19
"I Went to the Animal Fair" 25
"Little Arabella Miller" 31
"Little Bo Peep" .37
"Little Jack Horner" 42
"London Bridge" .46
"Mister Sun" 52
"The North Wind Doth Blow" 56
"Open Them, Shut Them" 63
"Peanut Butter and Jelly" 68
"There Was a Little Turtle 74
"Twinkle, Twinkle, Little Star" 81
"Two Little Apples" 87
"Where Is Thumbkin?" 93

Prediction

"Be Kind to Your Web-Footed Friends" 7
"The Eency Weency Spider" 15
"Humpty Dumpty" 19
"I Went to the Animal Fair" 25
"Little Arabella Miller" 31
"Little Bo Peep" .37
"Little Jack Horner" 42
"London Bridge" .46
"Mister Sun" 52
"The North Wind Doth Blow" 56
"Open Them, Shut Them" 63
"Peanut Butter and Jelly" 68
"There Was a Little Turtle 74
"Twinkle, Twinkle, Little Star" 81
"Two Little Apples" 87
"Where Is Thumbkin?" 93

Communication

"Be Kind to Your Web-Footed Friends" 7
"The Eency Weency Spider" 15
"Humpty Dumpty" 19
"I Went to the Animal Fair" 25
"Little Arabella Miller" 31
"Little Bo Peep" .37
"Little Jack Horner" 42
"London Bridge" .46
"Mister Sun" 52
"The North Wind Doth Blow" 56
"Open Them, Shut Them" 63
"Peanut Butter and Jelly" 68
"There Was a Little Turtle 74
"Twinkle, Twinkle, Little Star" 81
"Two Little Apples" 87
"Where Is Thumbkin?" 93

Dear Teacher or Parent,

How often have you said these words OK, everyone, time for circle time. Let's gather on the rug! and then thought to yourself "What should we do today?" This book will help you through those times when you are tired of the same old ideas. We've taken many familiar children's songs and created some great circle time activities for you to try. In addition, we'll give you ideas for originating your own songs, using these familiar tunes.

What is circle time?
Circle times are large or small group gatherings. During your circle time, you may present daily or weekly themes or concepts. You may use books, pictures, flannel boards, concrete materials, share experiences and sing songs!

What is the best way to do circle time?
There is no "best" way. Each teacher has his or her own style. You can gather ideas for your circle times by reading books, attending classes and observing other teachers. Eventually, you will develop your own style that works best for you and your class. Be aware that you may need to adjust your style from year to year, or even as the school year progresses, depending on the changes in your children.

Some circle time hints:
Establish a set place in your classroom to gather. It should be out of the room's main traffic pattern. A round or oval rug makes a great visual cue for the children as they come together. If possible, locate your circle time space near a window.

Have an easel, chalkboard or flannel board nearby for using visual aids or recording the children's ideas.

If you prefer a "backup" when you sing, use a tape, CD or record player. You don't need to be a great singer to have great circle times, but you will need to know how to use this equipment.

Plan your circle times for the same time each day. Children need a consistent schedule for each day's activities; they feel security in knowing the sequence of a day's planned events. Create a consistent pattern of activities within your circle time as well.

Name your circle time whatever you wish: morning meeting, group time, together time or something else unique to your children.

Use concrete items whatever possible.

If you find the children are not responding to a particular activity or song, STOP. Try again later on another day or in another way.

Sincerely,

Susan Karen

Susan Finkel and Karen Seberg

About This Book

Most studies show that science is an area in which U.S. students perform poorly compared to other countries. Parents and educators alike believe they could do a better job with the science curriculums in the schools. In many elementary classrooms, fewer than 20 minutes per day are spent on science. Obviously, science is a subject many teachers avoid when planning lessons or activities. And yet, many that need not be the case. Science is intensely interesting to children of this age and the scientific process—making predictions; looking for results, reactions or changes; drawing conclusions and evaluating what happened—is the foundation for a framework of lifelong learning.

The circle times in this book make it easy for you to give children those experiences using familiar children's songs. The activities for each song are organized by four scientific processes. They are:

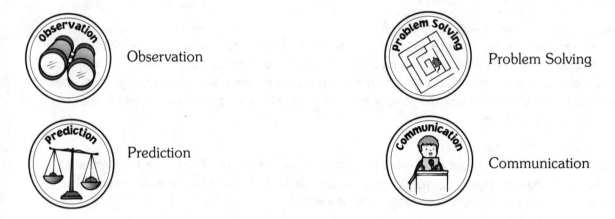

Observation

Prediction

Problem Solving

Communication

You can focus on one type of process to give your children experience with one skill at a time. You may also choose to use all four circle time activities and follow through with the four sequential processes on one related theme.

You will find yourself enjoying these science activities as you give your children an important opportunity to explore and experience basic scientific processes.

Be Kind to Your Web-Footed Friends

Be kind to your web-footed friends,
For a duck may be somebody's mother.
Be kind to your friends in the swamp,
Where the weather is always damp.
You may think that this is the end,
Well, it is!

Props/Visual Aids
You will need an instant camera.

Talk About
Have each child take off one shoe and sock. Remove your shoe and sock, too! Have the children carefully examine their feet. Ask, "What does your foot look like? Is it straight or bumpy, skinny or chubby? Is your ankle bony or smooth?" Take a photograph of each child's foot. Pass the pictures around the group. Can each child identify his or her own foot?

To Extend This Circle Time
Allow each child to make a row of footprints. You will want to inform parents of this activity ahead of time, and plan on working with only one or two children at a time. You will need a long strip of paper for each child (paper that comes on a roll would be ideal) and an aluminum cake pan with just enough washable paint to cover the bottom. Have a child remove shoes and socks and stand in the paint. Then help him or her to carefully walk the length of the paper. Have a tub of warm, soapy water and towels at the other end for immediate clean up. Display the footprints in a long, connecting strip around the perimeter of the room. Can the children identify which footprints are theirs?

Props/Visual Aids

Send home a note to parents asking them to trace around their own bare feet and return the tracings to school. During circle time, trace around each child's bare foot, using a washable marker.

Talk About

Measure and compare the feet of each member of the children's families. Ask, "Do you remember the last time you got new shoes? How did your feet feel in your old shoes? How did your new shoes feel? Why?" Use the tracings of the parents' feet to have children predict how big their feet will be when they are grown. With another color marker, draw the predicted size on the page with the child's actual foot tracing, showing how much the child's foot will need to grow to fulfill the prediction.

To Extend This Circle Time

Reproduce "When I have big feet, I will . . ." on page 11, making one for each child. What would it be like to have really big feet? Bring in as many really large pairs of shoes as you can find and invite the children to take turns wearing them. "How does it feel to have big feet? What will you be able to do when your feet really are this big?" Have the children draw pictures on the reproducible page.

Props/Visual Aids

Enlarge and reproduce the animal tracks and animal cards on page 12. Color and laminate for durability.

Talk About

Say, "Animals have many different kinds of feet. Some animals, like ducks and frogs have webbed feet to help them swim. Other animals, like cats and lions, have claws that scratch. Horses and deer have hooves that help them run fast." Share the picture cards of animals and their tracks. Help the children match the tracks to the animal that made them.

To Extend This Circle Time

Take the children on a nature walk to look for tracks. Can they discover what animal might have made the tracks they find? "Was the animal walking, running or hopping? How can you tell?" Partially fill your sensory table with damp sand. Have the children use craft sticks or twigs to make tracks in the sand. Have a partner determine what kind of tracks they might be.

Props/Visual Aids

Check your library for books on marsh and swamp habitats. Enlarge, reproduce, cut out and color the animal illustrations on pages 13 and 14. You will need two pieces of chart paper. Write *Web-Footed* (and make a simple drawing of a webbed foot) on one and label the other *Not Web-Footed*.

Talk About

Sing the song with the children. Share the books and illustrations of animals that live in a swamp or marsh. Say, "The song says be kind to your web-footed friends and be kind to your friends in the swamp. Do all of our friends in the swamp have webbed feet?" Look at the pictures carefully. Decide whether or not each animal has webbed feet and tape its picture to the corresponding chart.

Web-Footed	Not Web-Footed

To Extend This Circle Time

If possible, plan a field trip to a swamp or marshy area and observe the animals there. Check with local science or children's museums for exhibits on marsh habitats. Set up a miniature swamp in a terrarium. Transplant marsh plants and add several shallow dishes for ponds. You may choose to have some animals live in your marsh. Check with your pet store for care and feeding of any small animals–such as snails, turtles, frogs or snakes–that you may want to add and care for.

Books to Share

Dorros, Arthur. *Animal Tracks*. Scholastic, 1991.
> Watercolor paintings and a simple guessing game format introduce the tracks and signs left by various animals, including the raccoon, duck, frog, black bear and human.

Goor, Ron. *All Kinds of Feet*. Thomas Y. Crowell, 1984.
> Text and black and white photographs present the different types of feet found in the animal kingdom and describe how each type is suited to the needs of the animal to which it belongs.

James, Robert. *Feet*. Rourke Press, Inc., 1995.
> Colorful photographs accompany the simple text to discuss the anatomy of the human foot and information on foot problems, foot care and the feet of some animals.

Luenn, Nancy. *Squish! A Wetland Walk*. Atheneum, 1994.
> Simple, poetic text and watercolor paintings describe a child's enthusiastic explorations of a wetland, a place to look and listen; and a home for fish, birds and animals.

Stone, Lynn M. *Marshes and Swamps*. Childrens Press, 1983.
> Colorful photographs and simple text introduce the plants and animals that live in wetlands such as swamps, marshes and bogs, and emphasize the importance of wetlands to the Earth's ecology.

Yabuuchi, Masayuki. *Whose Footprints?* Philomel Books, 1985.
> Accurate paintings and very simple text depict the footprints of a monkey, duck, cat, horse, hippopotamus, bear and goat.

Resources

Mason, George F. *Animal Feet*. William Morrow and Company, 1970.
> Clear line drawings and simple, accurate text explain the adaptation to environment and anatomy of the feet of mammals, insects, lizards and birds.

Mason, George F. *Animal Tracks*. Linnet Books, 1988.
> This nature guide presents pictures of 44 North American animals, their tracks and footprints, from whitetail deer to the jackrabbit and house cat.

Silverstein, Alvin. *The Story of Your Foot*. G.P. Putnam's Sons, 1987.
> Describes the inside and outside story of the foot–its construction of bone, muscle, nerves, skin and nails, and the complex system that moves it.

Tapes and CDs

Beall, Pamela Conn, and Susan Hagen Nipp. "Be Kind to Your Web-Footed Friends" from *Wee Sing Silly Songs*. Price Stern Sloan, 1986.

Various Performers. "Be Kind to Your Web-Footed Friends" from *Disney's Silly Songs*. Walt Disney Records, 1988.

10

Name _____

When I have big feet, I will . . .

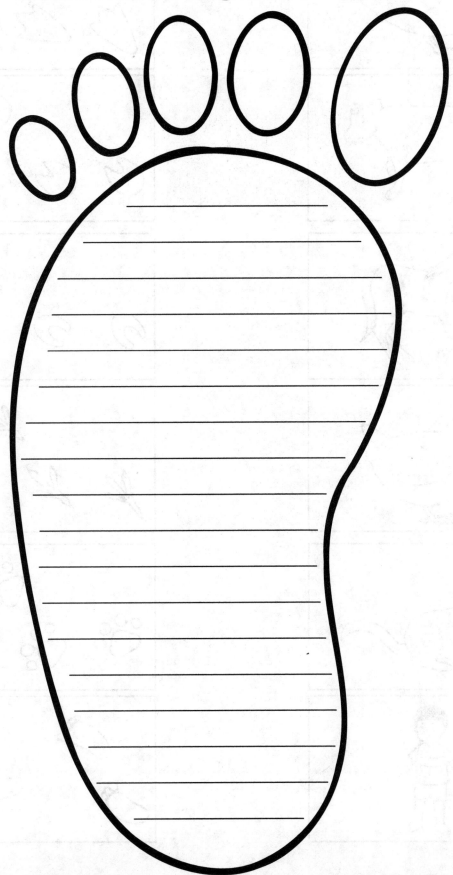

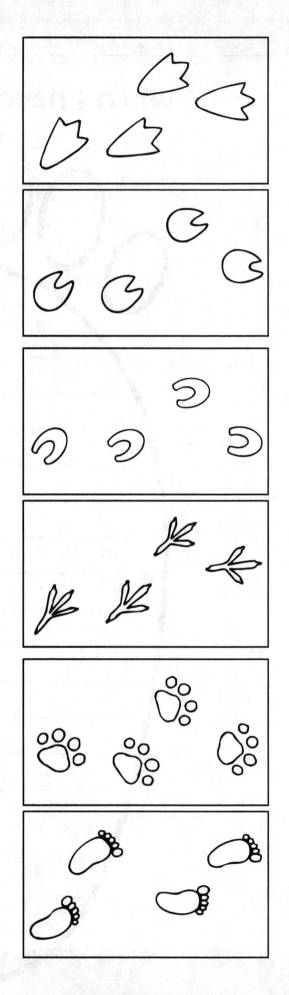

14

The Eency Weency Spider

The eency, weency spider went up the water spout.
Down came the rain and washed the spider out.
Out came the sun, and dried up all the rain,
So the eency weency spider went up the spout again.

Props/Visual Aids

You will need clear plastic peanut butter jars with lids. Use a sharp object to carefully poke small air holes in the bottom of the jar. Don't make them too large, or your spiders will escape!

Talk About

Go on a search of your classroom, playground or any good hiding place for spiders. When you spy a spider, determine that it is a harmless variety. Then carefully put the open end of the jar over it. Slide a piece of paper or cardboard under the spider to help scoop it into the jar and fasten the lid securely. You may want to add some twigs or grass for the spider to climb on. Share the spiders with the class. Watch them spin webs and find small live insects such as flies or moths to feed them.

To Extend This Circle Time

Different kinds of spiders spin different sorts of webs. Share books about spiders and their webs with your class. What types of webs did your spiders spin? Give each child a piece of black or brown paper and white chalk. Ask them to carefully observe the webs and then draw a web of their own.

Props/Visual Aids

You will need an empty aquarium with a lid, a small piece of PVC pipe or a tube for a hamster to play in available at pet stores and a few spiders.

Talk About

Place the pipe and spiders in the aquarium and replace the lid. Say, "The spiders in the song climbed up the water spout. Do you think our spiders will climb up the pipe? How long do you think it will take?" Record the children's predictions. Watch the spiders. Ask, "What would happen if we poured water down the pipe?"

To Extend This Circle Time

If available, set up a large expanding tunnel in your large muscle area. If your classroom does not have one, drape a sheet over a table. Have the children pretend to be spiders and crawl through the tunnel. Use white yarn to create a web in your classroom. Loosely wind the yarn around chairs, tables, doorknobs and other stable objects. Have your "spiders" crawl carefully through the web.

Props/Visual Aids

Find pictures of spiders and their webs. Make a yarn spiderweb on your flannel board. Cut out a spider and fly from the patterns on page 18 from gray or brown flannel and place them on the web. You will also need chart paper and markers.

Talk About

Say, "Some spiders catch their food with their sticky webs. What if you were a spider who couldn't spin a web? What would you have to do to catch this fly?" Discuss other ways animals get food. Some responses might be to chase it and capture it, hide and sneak up on it, learn to eat grass instead, grow wings or grow a long sticky tongue like a frog. List the children's ideas on chart paper and draw simple illustra-

tions of the changes of how the spider would look for each of the children's ideas.

To Extend This Circle Time

Make spiderwebs. Help the children glue two craft sticks together and allow the sticks to dry. Supply 2' to 3' (.61 to .91 ml) pieces of silver or gray yarn and invite the children to make "webs" by wrapping the yarn around the craft sticks. Add a small spider made with a black pom-pom body and strips of black construction paper for its legs.

Props/Visual Aids

You will need a large piece of chart paper and markers. Provide construction paper, crayons and washable markers for the children. Reproduce the spider patterns on page 18. Bring books about spiders to the circle.

Talk About

Spiders are really very helpful creatures, regardless of their bad reputations. Spiders eat many harmful insects. Share some of the information from your resource books and the spider pictures. Have the children help you make a list on large chart paper titled "Spiders Are Our Friends Because." When the list is completed, invite the children to make posters showing helpful spiders. Write captions for the children and display the posters in the room.

To Extend This Circle Time

Set your captured spider friends free! Outside is best, of course, if the season permits this. Try to find a spider-friendly spot if the original place of capture is not an option. Your class will have become fond of the creatures, so try to ensure their safety!

Books to Share

Freschet, Berniece. *The Web in the Grass*. Charles Scribner's Sons, 1972.
The little spider spins a silken web and an egg sac, and hides from her many enemies in this poetic story illustrated with colorful collages.

Gibbons, Gail. *Spiders*. Holiday House, 1993.
Colorful, clear illustrations and simple text examine the physical characteristics, behavior and habitats of different types of spiders.

Kirk, David. *Miss Spider's Tea Party*. Scholastic, 1994.
When lovely Miss Spider tries to host a tea party, the other bugs refuse to come for fear of being eaten.

Sardegna, Jill. *The Roly-Poly Spider*. Scholastic, 1994.
Told in verse with humorous illustrations, this story is about a very hungry spider who, after eating a bee, caterpillar, beetle and other insects, is too plump to go down the water spout.

Trapani, Iza. *The Itsy Bitsy Spider*. Whispering Coyote Press, 1993.
The itsy bitsy spider encounters a fan, a mouse, a rocking chair and a cat as she makes her way to the top of a tree to spin her web and rest in the sun.

Tapes and CDs

Beall, Pamela Conn, and Susan Hagen Nipp. "The Eensy Weensy Spider" from *Wee Sing Children's Songs and Fingerplays*. Price Stern Sloan, 1990.

Richard, Little. "Itsy Bitsy Spider" from *For Our Children*. Walt Disney Records, 1991.

Sharon, Lois and Bram. "The Eensy Weensy Spider" from *Great Big Hits*. A&M Records, Inc., 1992.

Humpty Dumpty

Humpty Dumpty sat on a wall.
Humpty Dumpty had a great fall.
All the king's horses and all the king's men
Couldn't put Humpty together again.

Observation

Props/Visual Aids
Try to find different types of real eggs (chicken, duck, dove, turtle, snake) or pictures of a variety of eggs to share with the class.

Talk About
Traditionally, Humpty Dumpty has been illustrated as an egg. Ask, "Can you think of different animals that hatch from eggs?" (You may choose to include only the animals that hatch from eggs outside their mothers' bodies. If your group is older, you may want to discuss animals that grow from eggs inside their mothers' bodies.) Share with the children the real eggs or the pictures of a variety of eggs. "How are these eggs different from each other? What kind of egg do you think this is? What might grow inside this egg?"

To Extend This Circle Time
Humpty Dumpty fell off the wall because of the forces of gravity. Set up a situation in your classroom where the children can safely experience gravity. Have a child sit on a low wall or stack of blocks and then fall into a pile of large, soft pillows and cushions. Sing the song as the child sits and "falls." The children who have had a turn can be the king's horses and men and help the child up. To ensure safety and no bumped heads, be sure that only one child plays Humpty Dumpty at a time.

Prediction

Props/Visual Aids
Reproduce the egg and animal patterns on pages 22 and 23. Make one egg for each animal. Color and laminate the pieces for durability. Fasten the halves of the egg together with a paper fastener. Hide the baby animal behind the egg and open the halves to show the animal. You could also use the plastic eggs available at Easter, placing a plastic animal inside, or the paper animals from pages 22 and 23.

Talk About
Show the closed eggs to the children. Ask, "Can you guess what baby animal is inside this egg? What do you think is going to hatch?" Give clues to help the children predict what animal is inside. "This animal likes to swim, but it can crawl on the land, too. It has a shell. Yes, a turtle!" Open the egg to show the animal inside. Provide enough egg patterns for each child to color and take home their own eggs.

To Extend This Circle Time

Borrow an incubator and try to hatch some eggs. Check with a local hatchery to purchase fertilized eggs. You may want to explain to the children that these eggs are not the same as eggs their parents purchase from the grocery store. Count the days on the calendar and have the children predict when the eggs will hatch. Don't allow the eggs to incubate too far past their due date, and dispose of unhatched eggs carefully. Be sure to have homes for the animals when they hatch. Some hatcheries will take back any hatched chickens.

Problem Solving

Props/Visual Aids

You will need plastic eggs such as the ones available at Easter. Have an assortment of pillows, baskets and scarves for the children's experimentation.

Talk About

Say, "When Humpty Dumpty fell, he broke! What are some ways you could have saved him?" Listen to the children's suggestions which may include wearing a seat belt, falling on a pillow or someone catching him on the ground. Invite the children to roll plastic eggs off a table or low bookshelf. Ask, "How could you keep the eggs from breaking? What could the eggs fall on or in so they won't break? Can a partner catch the egg so it will not hit the floor?"

To Extend This Circle Time

Use the egg patterns on page 24 to make egg puzzles. You will need washable markers or crayons, safety scissors and folders for each of the children's puzzle pieces. Have each child decorate an egg and help him or her cut it into four pieces. You may want to cut the egg into more pieces for older children. Write the child's name on the back of each puzzle piece. Ask, "Can you put Humpty Dumpty together again?" Store the pieces in stapled paper pocket folders or envelopes to take home.

Props/Visual Aids

You will need chart paper and markers.

Talk About

Say, "Poor Humpty! Too bad he didn't know the rules about sitting on the wall. What do you think those rules for staying safe on the wall might be?" Listen to the children's responses and write them on the chart paper with a simple illustration. You might write: *Don't wiggle. Don't stand up. Hold on to your mom's hand. Wear your seat belt.*

To Extend This Circle Time

Have the children make "before" and "after" pictures of Humpty Dumpty. Provide construction paper scraps, glue, washable markers or crayons and pieces of eggshell which have been dyed in food coloring. Give each child a copy of the egg pattern on page 24. To make the "before" picture, children can add facial features, arms, legs and clothing to their eggs. Then have them glue on pieces of broken, colored eggshell for the "after" picture.

Books to Share

Burton, Jane, and Robert Burton. *Egg.* Dorling Kindersley, 1994.
    Close-up photographs capture the moment of hatching, from the first tiny crack in the eggshell to the newborn bursting free, of a variety of birds, reptiles, fish and insects.

Cole, Joanna. *A Chick Hatches.* Morrow Junior Books, 1976.
    Black and white photographs and simple text tell the story of what happens inside a chicken egg during its 21-day incubation.

Hariton, Anca. *Egg Story.* Dutton Children's Books, 1992.
    From a white spot on a yolk to a wet and weary chick that has struggled out of its shell, each stage of growth inside the egg is simply and accurately presented in text and pictures.

Heller, Ruth. *Chickens Aren't the Only Ones.* Grosset &d Dunlap, 1981.
    Detailed, colorful drawings and rhyming text show many birds, reptiles, fish and insects who lay eggs.

Selsam, Millicent. *All About Eggs.* Addison-Wesley, 1980.
    Simple text and clear drawings describe the different kinds of eggs, some of which we cannot see inside the mother, and all the different creatures that grow from them.

Tapes and CDs

Barolk Folk with Madeline MacNeil and Barbara Hess. "Humpty Dumpty" from *Girls and Boys Come Out to Play.* Music for Little People, 1991.

King's Singers, The. "Humpty Dumpty" from *Kids' Stuff.* EMI Records, Ltd., 1986.

Various Performers. "Humpty Dumpty" from *Family Folk Festival: A Multicultural Sing-Along.* Music for Little People, 1990.

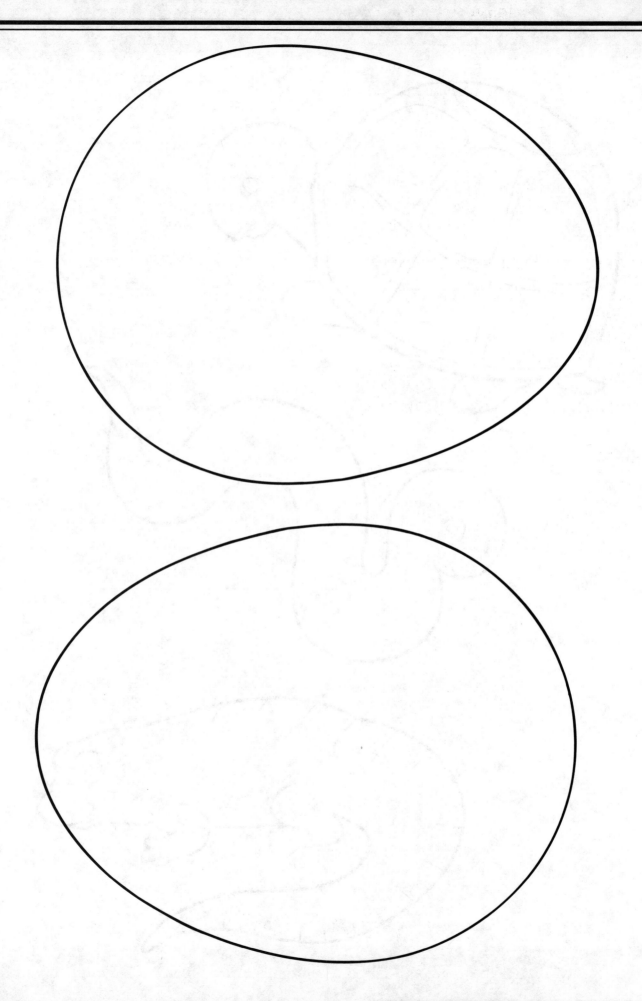

24

I Went to the Animal Fair

I went to the animal fair.
The birds and the beasts were there.
The big baboon by the light of the moon,
Was combing his auburn hair.
You should have seen the monk,
He sat on the elephant's trunk,
The elephant sneezed and fell on his knees,
And what became of the monk, the monk?

Props/Visual Aids
You will need a set of dominoes or wooden or cardboard rectangular blocks. If you have younger children in your group, you will find it easier to work with the blocks.

Talk About
This song describes a chain reaction. An action takes place, which causes the following action and so on. You can illustrate a simple chain reaction by setting the dominoes or blocks on end in a row. When the end domino is knocked over, it strikes the next, and the reaction continues down the line. Give each child five dominoes to set up his or her own chain reaction. Then invite them to work in groups to create longer chains. Can the whole class make a row of dominoes all the way down the hall?

To Extend This Circle Time
Many cartoons, old movies and classic TV shows illustrate comical chain reactions. Check with your local video store for some examples. Share an age-appropriate clip with your class. Try watching it in slow motion or pausing every few frames to catch the action as it happens.

Props/Visual Aids

Enlarge, reproduce and color the picture cards on pages 28 and 29. You will also need chart paper and markers.

Talk About

Prediction is guessing "what will happen next?" Say, "What do you think happened to the monkey when the elephant sneezed?" Show the children each of the picture cards. Have them guess what might happen next in each situation. Encourage lots of varied responses and record the ideas on chart paper. Try setting up some of the picture card situations to see what will happen.

To Extend This Circle Time

Play a game throughout the day. Call it Stop! What Happens Next? At different times during the day, call out the phrase. Have everyone freeze and then ask the children, "What happens next?"

Props/Visual Aids

Reproduce the "What Became of the Monk?" pattern on page 30. Make one for each child and provide crayons or washable markers. You will also need a monkey doll or puppet.

Talk About

What did happen to the monkey when the elephant sneezed? Tell the children that today they will have a special visitor. Introduce the monkey doll by name, and describe it as the monkey in the song. If you are not comfortable talking for the monkey and using a monkey voice, have the monkey whisper answers to you. Encourage the children to ask the monkey questions, such as "Why did you sit on the elephant's trunk? How did you get up there? What happened to you when the elephant sneezed?" Give each child the monkey page. As they color their monkeys, go around the class, writing their responses to the question on the page.

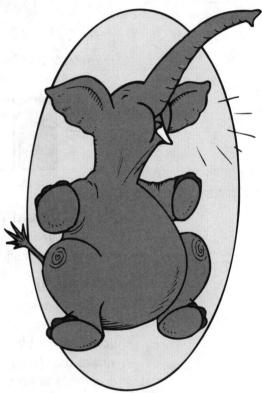

To Extend This Circle Time

Ask, "Why do you think the elephant sneezed?" Some responses might be that he had a cold, he was allergic to monkeys, it was dusty at the fair. "Sneezes can spread germs and are catching. What should the elephant have done when he sneezed?" Invite the children to act out sneezing into a tissue or covering their noses with their arms. Play a chain reaction game where each child sneezes in turn, while covering his or her nose and mouth. When the sneezes have made the full circle, have everyone join in one elephant-sized sneeze!

Props/Visual Aids

You will need several sheets of chart paper and markers. Label the pages "Things I Did," "Things I Saw and Heard" and "Things I Ate and Drank." Whenever possible throughout the activity, add a simple drawing under the words for a visual clue.

Talk About

Say, "This song is about an animal fair. Have any of you ever been to a carnival or fair? What did you see there? What was your favorite thing to do at the fair?" List the children's responses on the chart paper, adding stars or checks to the answers that are repeated several times. Then look at the completed charts and help summarize the children's experiences. "Wow! Five of us like to eat corn dogs at the fair, and nine of us like snow cones!"

To Extend This Circle Time

Stage your own animal fair. Invite the children to bring their favorite stuffed animals. Decorate with balloons and play carnival or calliope music. Play games such as ring toss and fishing with magnets for fish on paper clips. Join hands in a circle to make a merry-go-round. Enjoy popcorn and juice at the fair.

Books to Share

Aardema, Verna. *Why Mosquitoes Buzz in People's Ears*. Dial Press, 1975.
   This colorfully illustrated folktale from West Africa relates a chain of events that finally reveal the meaning of the mosquitos buzz.

Gibbons, Gail. *Country Fair*. Little, Brown and Company, 1994.
   Bright watercolors illustrate this account of a country fair, from the first tent stake driven into the ground to the crowded midway, the livestock judging and finally to the evening's fireworks.

Hansard, Peter. *I Like Monkeys Because . . .* Candlewick Press, 1993.
   Simple text illustrated with watercolor paintings describe a variety of monkeys and apes around the world and some of the interesting things they do.

Stevens, Janet. *Animal Fair*. Holiday House, 1981.
   In this retelling of the traditional song, a little boy is awakened by a friendly panda who takes him to the animal fair.

Tafuri, Nancy. *This Is the Farmer*. Greenwillow Books, 1994.
   Full-page illustrations and very simple text relate an amusing chain of events on a farm that begins when the farmer kisses his wife.

Tapes and CDs

Beall, Pamela Conn, and Susan Hagen Nipp. "Animal Fair" from *Wee Sing Silly Songs*. Price Stern Sloan, 1986.

Monet, Lisa. "Animal Fair" from *Jump Down*. Circle Sound Productions, 1987.

Roth, Kevin. "Animal Fair" from *Oscar, Bingo and Buddies*. CMS Records, Inc., 1986.

Various Performers. "Animal Fair" from *Disney's Children's Favorites, Vol. 1*. Walt Disney Productions, 1979.

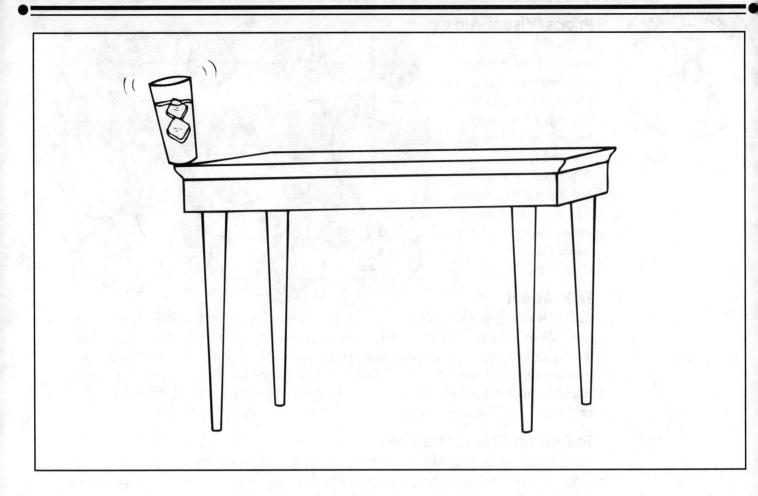

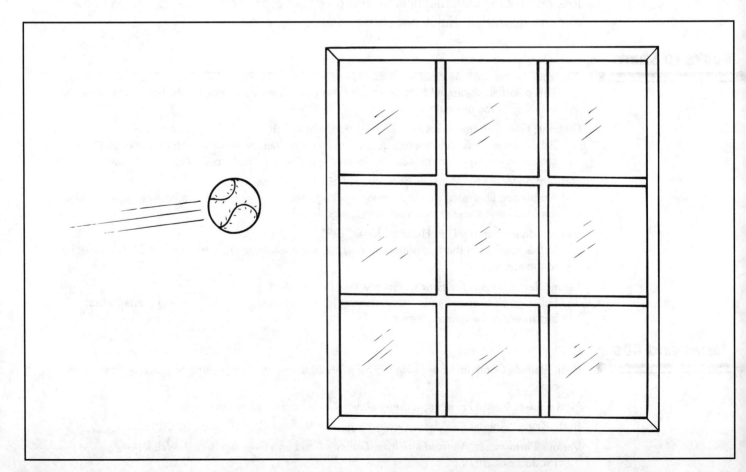

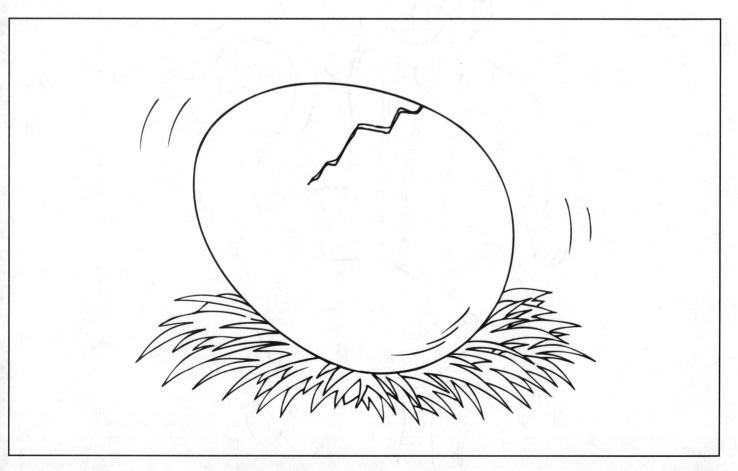

What Became of the Monk?

_____

_____

_____

_____

_____

_____

Little Arabella Miller

(To the tune of "Twinkle, Twinkle, Little Star")

Little Arabella Miller
Found a woolly caterpillar.
First it crawled upon her mother,
Then upon her baby brother.
All said, "Arabella Miller,
Take away that caterpillar!"

Props/Visual Aids

Find pictures of caterpillars from resource books or nature magazines. You will also need washable markers, washable paint or tempera paint in a variety of colors (to which a few drops of liquid soap has been added) and cotton swabs. You will want to inform parents in advance of this activity.

Talk About

Caterpillars are creepy crawly! Share the pictures of caterpillars with the children. Ask, "Have you ever seen a caterpillar? What did it look like?" Invite the children to decorate their pointer finger to look like a caterpillar. Using the cotton swabs as brushes, have the children paint the finger of their nondominant hand. It will be easier for them to control their painting as well as interfere less with the rest of the day's activities. Children can move their caterpillar fingers all day.

To Extend This Circle Time

Provide your art center with cardboard egg cartons cut lengthwise into two six-cup sections, pipe cleaners, tempera paint and brushes. Children can decorate the sections to resemble caterpillars and add pipe cleaner legs or antennae.

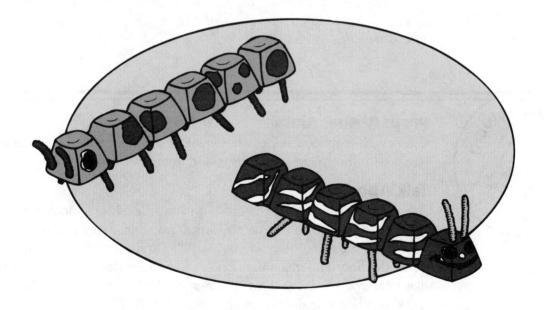

Props/Visual Aids

Enlarge and reproduce the life cycle patterns on page 35. Use a piece of rolled masking tape on each card to help it adhere to the flannel board. You may wish to code the pieces to keep the cards in the correct insect's life cycle.

Talk About

Say, "There are many different kinds of butterflies and moths, but each starts from a tiny egg." Show the children one of the egg cards. Ask, "What do you think will hatch from this egg?" Display the caterpillar card for that insect and continue asking the children to predict what stage of the life cycle is next. "Do you think a moth or a butterfly is inside this cocoon?" Continue with the other life cycle cards.

To Extend This Circle Time

Invite the children to make pupa finger puppets. Mix a drop or two of washable green paint into white glue. Use a brush to paint a thin coat of the mixture on the child's nondominant pointer finger. As the glue mixture dries, the finger will stiffen slightly. Some children may dislike the sensation of the glue mixture on their fingers.

Props/Visual Aids

Check with your local library for videotapes on caterpillars and butterflies. Share books with the children on insects and their life cycles.

Talk About

Ask, "How did the caterpillar crawl on Arabella Miller's mother and brother?" Show the children a video about caterpillars, if possible, and share books about them. If your climate permits, find a real caterpillar and watch it move. Invite the children to lie on the floor and move their bodies like caterpillars. Ask, "Can one person look like a caterpillar? What if two or three people work together? Can the whole class work together to make one really long caterpillar?"

32

To Extend This Circle Time

Use the patterns on page 36 to make butterfly finger puppets. Provide each child with a butterfly, washable markers or crayons, glue and safety scissors. You may want to help younger children cut out their butterflies. Cut strips of paper, 1/2" x 3" (1.25 x 8 cm). Tape the strip to fit around a child's pointer finger, and glue the butterfly's body to the strip. When the child moves his or her hand, the butterfly's wings will flutter.

Communication

Props/Visual Aids

You will need multicolored nylon scarves or pieces of fabric.

Talk About

Invite the children to act out the life cycle of a butterfly. First, have them curl up as eggs, then crawl like caterpillars, wrap up in the scarves like cocoons, then fly with scarves for butterfly wings. Videotape the performance with narration and classical background music. Invite another class to see the show and share the video with parents.

To Extend This Circle Time

Make a butterfly snack. Cut a bagel in half lengthwise and then in half again to make two half circles. Rotate the pieces so the curved sides touch. Spread cream cheese on the bagel, using different flavors or food coloring tints and place a pretzel stick in the center for the butterfly's body.

Books to Share

Carle, Eric. *The Very Hungry Caterpillar*. Philomel Books, 1969.
Illustrated with colorful collages, a hungry little caterpillar eats through a very large quantity of food until, full at last, he spins a cocoon, goes to sleep and wakes up a butterfly.

Cutts, David. *Look . . . a Butterfly*. Troll Associates, 1982.
Detailed, accurate illustrations and very simple text follow the development of a variety of butterflies from egg through caterpillar and cocoon to maturity.

Hariton, Anca. *Butterfly Story*. Dutton Children's Books, 1995.
Simple text and delicate and accurate illustrations tell of the dramatic cycle of egg to caterpillar, caterpillar to pupa and finally, the transformation to butterfly.

Ring, Elizabeth. *Night Flier*. Millbrook Press, 1994.
Lyrical text and exceptional close-up photographs combine to create a unique presentation of the life cycle of the cecropia moth.

Taylor, Kim. *Butterfly*. Dorling Kindersley, 1992.
Clear photographs and simple text follow a butterfly's growth from a tiny egg to a full-grown caterpillar which becomes a chrysalis and finally emerges as the beautiful butterfly.

Tapes and CDs

Carfra, Pat. "Little Arabella Miller" from *Songs for Sleepyheads and Out-of-Beds!* Lullaby Lady Productions, 1984.

Feldman, Ellen. "Little Arabella Miller" from *Razzama Tazzama*. Ellen Feldman, 1989.

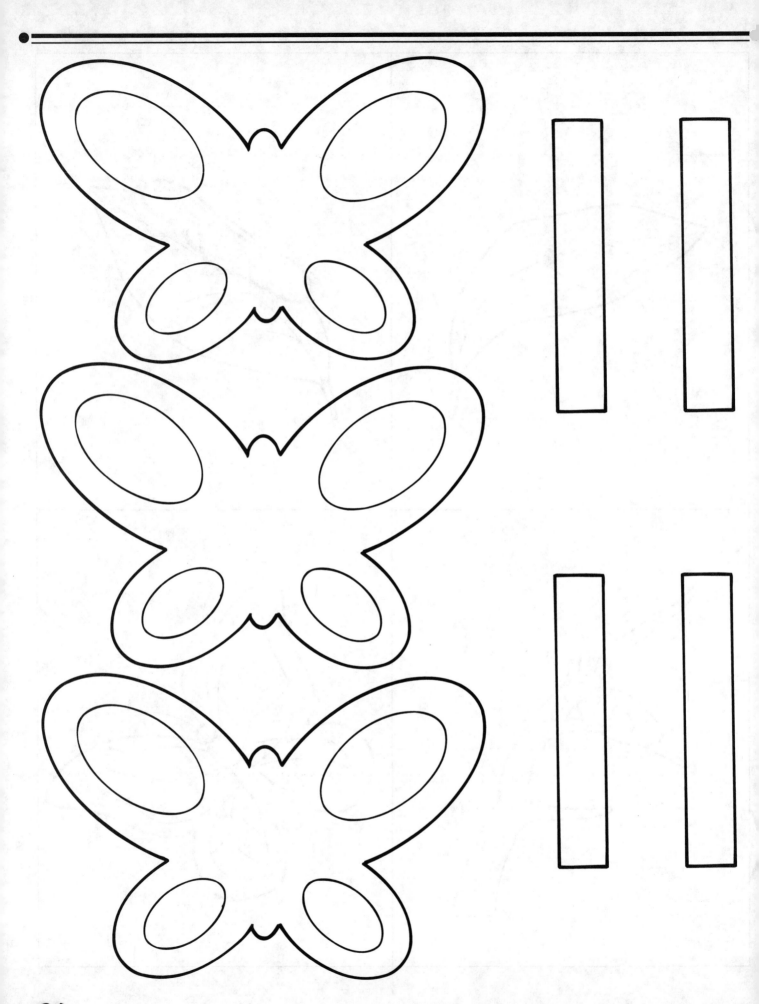

36

Little Bo Peep

Little Bo Peep has lost her sheep
And can't tell where to find them.
Leave them alone, and they'll come home,
And bring their tails behind them.

Observation

Props/Visual Aids

Share with the children a variety of books with pictures of animals, especially focusing on the different types of animal tails. If possible, view a nature video showing many types of animals. Enlarge, color, cut out and laminate the animal tails on page 40.

Talk About

As you look at the animal books or view the video, discuss the variety of tails the animals have. Show the children the tails you have made. Help them identify the animal to which each tail belongs. Ask how each animal uses its tail and invite the children to demonstrate. Vary the words to the song to include each type of animal and tail. You might sing, "Little Bo Peep has lost her pigs." Older children will enjoy changing Bo Peep's name to rhyme with the name of the lost animal. "Little Bo Porse has lost her horse."

To Extend This Circle Time

Go for a walk around the neighborhood or take a field trip to a park, zoo or farm. Look for the animals that live there and observe how different animals use their tails.

Prediction

Props/Visual Aids

You will need cotton balls, chart paper and markers.

Talk About

Hide cotton ball "sheep" around the room. Designate an area or box to be the pen for the found sheep. Say, "Bo Peep has lost 20 sheep! If you were a lost sheep, where would you hide? How long do you think it will take to find all 20 sheep?" Keep track of the time as the children search for the lost sheep. Record the prediction and actual time on the chart paper. Then repeat the activity with more or fewer sheep. "How long do you think it will take to find 10 sheep?"

To Extend This Circle Time

Act out the rhyme. Choose one child (or several, if your group is large) to be Bo Peep and the rest of the children "hide" throughout the room. Talk about the places the sheep might be. "Is the block area where the best grass is? Where can the sheep get good water to drink?" Have the sheep follow Bo Peep back to the circle time area, and play again with a new cast of characters.

Props/Visual Aids

Reproduce the animal tail patterns on page 40. Make enough so that each child will have two or three, and hide the tails around the classroom.

Talk About

"Bo Peep has lost her sheep and a lot of other animals besides! And all of the animals have lost their tails! What a mess!" Invite the children to search the classroom to find the missing tails. You may want to write clues to help the children search. For example, if you have hidden the pig's tail in the sandbox, you could say, "My tail is where you like to dig. It is curly and twirly, because I'm a pig!" Have the children bring all of the tails to the circle time area. Ask, "Which tail belongs to the sheep? Which belongs to the pig? How can you tell?"

To Extend This Circle Time

Ask the children if they have ever wanted to have a tail. "What kind of tail would you like? How would it feel? How would you use it? "Provide your art center with a variety of materials and invite the children to make tails. You might use cardboard tubes (short and long), net sponges, nylons, yarn, paper scraps and newspapers. Carefully fasten each child's tail to his or her clothing with a safety pin. Don't forget to make a tail for yourself!

Communication

Props/Visual Aids
Reproduce one Lost/Found posters on page 41 for each child. Provide washable markers or crayons.

Talk About
Ask, "What can Bo Peep do to try to find her sheep?" Listen to and discuss the children's responses. If no one suggests it, say, "Sometimes when people lose things, they make and put up posters to show others what they lost." Then ask, "How do you think Bo Peep will feel when she finds her sheep? What should she do after she finds them?" Give each child a Lost/Found page and markers or crayons. Invite them to pretend to be Bo Peep making a poster to help find her lost sheep. What should they draw? Then have the children pretend to find their sheep and draw another poster depicting the found sheep.

To Extend This Circle Time
Use the Lost/Found posters on page 41 for your classroom lost and found box. If a child loses an item, he or she can make a poster to advertise its loss. A child who finds a lost item can make another poster.

Books to Share
Brown, Marc Tolon. *The Silly Tail Book.* Parents' Magazine Press, 1983.
  Humorous illustrations and rhyming text describe what tails are and aren't, what they can and can't do, where they grow and don't.

Kiser, Kevin. *Sherman the Sheep.* Macmillan, 1994.
  A flock of adventurous sheep follow Sherman, the smartest sheep in the field, on a long journey to find the best field in the whole valley, which turns out to have been home all along.

Lewis, Kim. *Emma's Lamb.* Four Winds Press, 1991.
  Detailed illustrations help tell the story of Emma's lamb, who becomes lost and is finally reunited with his mother.

Potter, Tessa. *Sheep.* Steck-Vaughn, 1990.
  Colorful photographs and simple text describe the lives of sheep on a farm and uses of the wool from their fleece.

Royston, Angela. *Lamb.* Lodestar Books, 1992.
  Clear photographs and very simple text depict the growth and development of a lamb from its first hour of life to 12 weeks old.

Shaw, Nancy. *Sheep Take a Hike.* Houghton Mifflin, 1994.
  Colorful illustrations and rhyming text tell of a flock of sheep who become lost on a chaotic hike and then find their way back following the trail of wool they have left.

Resources
Zappler, Lisbeth. *The Natural History of the Tail.* Doubleday and Company, 1972.
  A humorous, yet scientifically accurate tour of the variety of tails found in the animal kingdom and their many uses.

Tapes and CDs
Rashad, Phylicia. "Little Bo Peep" from *Baby's Nursery Rhymes.* Lightyear Records, 1991.

Rosenthal, Phil. "Little Bo Peep" from *Comin' Round the Mountain.* American Melody, 1993.

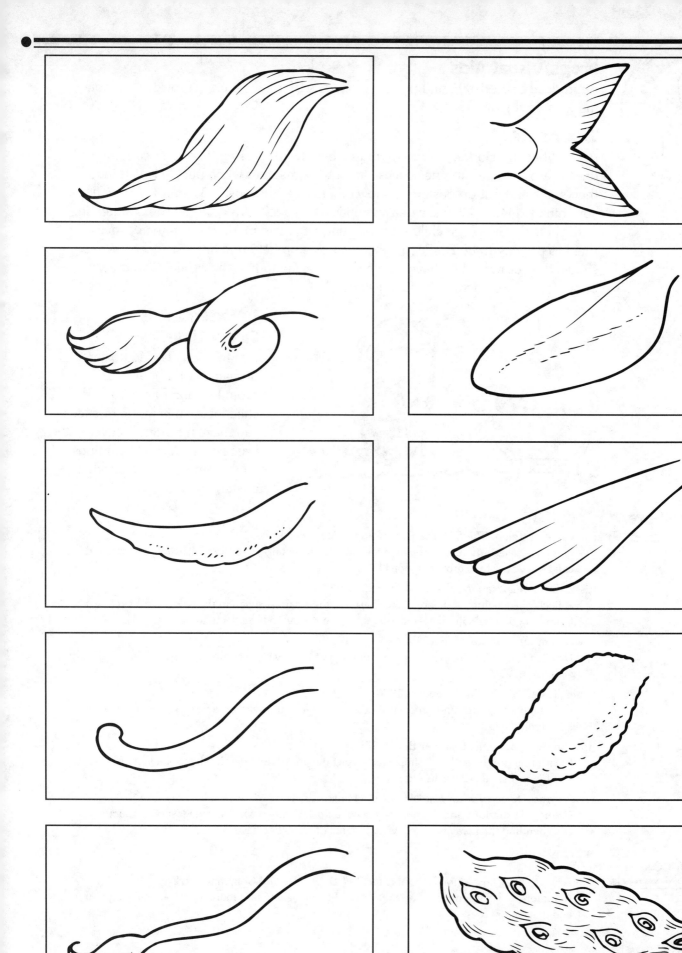

Lost

Found

Little Jack Horner

Little Jack Horner
Sat in a corner
Eating his Christmas pie.
He put in his thumb
And pulled out a plum
And said, "What a good boy am I!"

Props/Visual Aids

Fasten two aluminum pie tins together on one side so that the top of one tin closes down on the top of the other. Find a variety of small items to put inside, one for each child in your class. You will also need chart paper and markers.

Talk About

Say, "Little Jack Horner was lucky to have found a plum in his pie. What are some other things that would fit in a pie?" Write the children's responses on the chart paper. Then show them your pie. Invite each child to reach in and pull out an item. Sing the song, varying the words to include the name of the child and the item they selected from the pie. You might sing, "Little Chad Remmel . . . and pulled out a spool!"

To Extend This Circle Time

Bring to class several kinds of plums. Allow the children to examine the fruit. Ask, "How are these plums alike? How are they different?" Then show the children some prunes. "How is the prune different than the plums?" Wash and cut the fruit so that the children may have a taste of each.

Props/Visual Aids

Use a black marker to trace around a variety of common classroom objects. You will also need a sock and several small items to put inside. You might have a marble, a toothbrush and a penny.

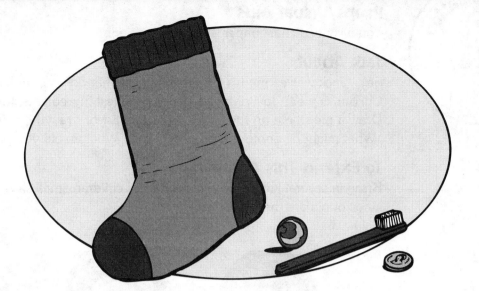

Talk About

Say, "Jack didn't know what he was going to pull out of the pie. When he stuck his thumb in, he probably thought, 'What is this? It feels like a . . .'" Let the children describe what the plum might have felt like. Then ask each child to put his or her hand in the sock and use only the sense of touch to identify the objects. Show the children the tracings. Ask if anyone can tell what object the outlines represent.

To Extend This Circle Time

Have the children identify other objects in the classroom using only one of their senses. You might play a recording of sound effects for them to recognize. Use 35 mm film canisters to make containers to smell. Puncture holes in the lids and put cotton balls that have been saturated with the desired smells in the containers. Have the children wear blindfolds to taste different food items.

Props/Visual Aids

Reproduce the patterns of fruit and seed cards on page 45. Color them realistically and laminate for durability. Bring in a variety of real fruit. You will need a plastic knife to cut into the fruit to find the seeds.

Talk About

Say, "Jack pulled a plum out of his pie. Do you think he found a seed in it?" Show the children a real plum and cut it open to find the seed or pit. Pass the seed around. Ask, "What does the seed feel like? How does it smell?" Show the pattern cards of fruits and seeds. Have the children match the seed card to the fruit. Cut apart the real fruit and find the seeds to help them discover which belong together.

To Extend This Circle Time

Use a food dehydrator to dry different kinds of fruit or purchase some commonly dried fruits available commercially. Have the children compare the dried fruit and fresh fruit. Try drying some seeds. Does drying a seed change its appearance? Ask, "Do you think the dried seed will still grow?"

Communication

Props/Visual Aids

You will need chart paper and markers.

Talk About

Say, "Jack was eating his Christmas pie. What do you think should be in a Christmas pie?" Invite the children to suggest ingredients, the sillier the better. Draw a pie shape on the chart paper and list or draw the children's responses. "What might be another kind of silly pie? What would you put in a science pie?"

To Extend This Circle Time

Bring in several kinds of pie and give the children small samples of each. Which kinds of pie are their favorites?

Books to Share

Cole, Joanna. *You Can't Smell a Flower with Your Ear! All About Your 5 Senses.* Grosset & Dunlap, 1994.
Describes how each of the five sense organs works, and includes an experiment to try for each one of the senses.

Fowler, Allan. *Feeling Things.* Children's Press, 1991.
Clear photographs illustrate and simple text discusses the sense of touch and how it works to tell us more about the world around us.

McMillan, Bruce. *Sense Suspense: A Guessing Game for the Five Senses.* Scholastic, 1994.
Colorful close-up photographs of objects on a Caribbean island invite children to decide which of their five senses they would be most likely to use; can it be touched, heard, seen, smelled or tasted?

Miller, Margaret. *My Five Senses.* Simon & Schuster Books for Young Readers, 1994.
Colorful photographs of children and very simple text introduce the five senses and how they help us experience the world around us.

Otto, Carolyn. *I Can Tell by Touching.* HarperCollins, 1994.
Simple, rhythmic text and lively illustrations explain how the sense of touch helps to identify everyday objects and familiar surroundings.

Tapes and CDs

Glazer, Tom. "Little Jack Horner" from *Tom Glazer Sings Winnie the Pooh and Mother Goose.* Gateway Records, RTV Communications Group, Inc., 1991.

Ives, Burl. "Little Jack Horner" from *Little White Duck and Other Children's Favorites.* Columbia, 1974.

London Bridge

London Bridge is falling down,
Falling down, falling down.
London Bridge is falling down,
My fair lady.
(verses)
Build it up with wood and clay . . .
Wood and clay will wash away . . .
Build it up with bricks and mortar . . .
Bricks and mortar will not stay . . .
Build it up with iron and steel . . .
Iron and steel will bend and bow . . .

Props/Visual Aids

You will need pictures of a variety of types of bridges. You may wish to enlarge the pictures of bridges on page 50 to share with the class.

Talk About

Sing the song with the children. Look carefully at the pictures of bridges. Compare a bridge to the illustrations and decide what type of bridge it is. Vary the words to the song to sing about different types of bridges and the materials from which they were constructed. You might sing, "The suspension bridge is falling down . . . Build it up with rope and wood . . ."

To Extend This Circle Time

Take a walking field trip to explore any bridges in your neighborhood. If there are different types of bridges in your communtiy, plan a field trip or take photographs of the bridges to share with the class. Can the children identify the types of bridges that they see?

Props/Visual Aids

From blue felt or construction paper, cut out several rivers in a variety of widths. Use the patterns on page 51 to cut out logs and rocks from brown and gray felt or construction paper.

Talk About

Put one of the blue felt rivers on the flannel board and arrange the rocks and logs to one side. Say, "We need to build a bridge to cross this river. Here are some logs. How many logs do you think we will need to make the bridge go all the way across?" After the children have made their predictions, ask a child to build the bridge. Repeat the activity with the other rivers and rocks.

To Extend This Circle Time

Make bridges you can eat! Prepare blue gelatin and give each child a rectangular-shaped serving. Give the children small pretzel sticks and pieces of graham cracker squares to build bridges across their gelatin "rivers." After the construction project, enjoy your snack!

Props/Visual Aids

You will need a variety of materials to build small bridges in your classroom. You might want craft sticks cut into varying lengths, cereal boxes with one side cut out, shoe boxes with lids and masking tape.

TLC10065 Copyright © Teaching & Learning Company, Carthage, IL 62321

Talk About

Building a bridge involves many problem-solving skills. Where is the best place to build it? How long does the bridge need to be? How strong does the bridge have to be? Say, "We are going to pretend that we are very, very tiny. Let's sing the song in our very, very tiny voices." Go for a walk as tiny people, using your pointer and middle fingers as legs. Talk in tiny voices and make up stories about what you see. "Here we go up this big hill (up a chair leg) and across the mountain and down the other side." Finally, you come to a river. "Oh, no! How can we get across?" Listen to the children's responses, and lead them, if necessary, to the idea of building a bridge. Work with the materials you have supplied and any others the children choose from the classroom. Ask questions as the children work. "How long do the boards need to be? What if they aren't big enough? What else can you use?"

To Extend This Circle Time

Continue this game in your sensory table with sand and "rivers" in dishpans or other elongated containers or out on the playground. Children love to go on adventures. Don't forget to take provisions and supplies in your backpack!

Props/Visual Aids

You will need pictures of a variety of types of bridges. You may wish to enlarge the pictures of bridges on page 50. You will also need chart paper and markers.

Talk About

Sing the song with the class. As the different building materials are described, list them on the chart paper. Have the children help you match the pictures of bridges to the building materials in the song. Say, "What does the song say will happen if we build a bridge with wood? Bricks? What are the best and strongest materials to build with in the song? Do you think the song is right?" Ask the children to think of some other building materials for bridges and decide if they would make strong bridges. Use their ideas to create new verses for the song.

To Extend This Circle Time

Divide into groups and play the traditional game that follows the song. This is one of the many versions of the game. Choose two children to be the "bridge." Have them face one another and join hands to make an arch. The other children form a line and run under the arch while singing the song. When "my fair lady" is sung, the bridge is dropped, capturing one of the children. Rock the child back and forth while singing, "take the key and lock him or her up!" The child is then taken aside while singing, "off to prison he or she must go!" The game continues until all the children have been captured.

Books to Share

Carlisle, Norman, and Madelyn Carlisle. *Bridges*. Children's Press, 1983.
> Clear, color photographs illustrate and simple text discusses the first bridges, famous and unusual bridges, and bridge design and construction.

Emberley, Ed. *London Bridge Is Falling Down: The Song and Game*. Little, Brown and Company, 1967.
> Whimsical ink drawings illustrate the familiar song, with music and instructions for playing a game with the verses included.

Robbins, Ken. *Bridges*. Dial Books, 1991.
> Hand-colored photographs show many different types of bridges with descriptions of their design and use.

Sheppard, Jeff. *I Know a Bridge*. Macmillan Publishing Company, 1993.
> Very simple text and colorful paintings present various kinds of bridges, from a steel bridge for trains, to a stone bridge for cars, old bridges and new.

Spier, Peter. *London Bridge Is Falling Down!* Doubleday, 1967.
> Detailed ink and watercolor illustrations interpret the verses to the song along with the music and a short history of London Bridge from 43 B.C. to the present.

Resources

Carter, Polly. *The Bridge Book*. Simon & Schuster Books for Young Readers, 1992.
> Simple and accurate line drawings and text describe the history of bridges, various kinds of bridges and how they are constructed.

Tapes and CDs

Greenberg, Josh. "London Bridge" from *Rhythm and Rhymes*. A Gentle Wind, Inc., 1982.

McGrath, Bob. "London Bridge" from *Sing Along with Bob, Vol. 2*. Kids' Records, 1985.

Various Performers. "London Bridge" from *Disney's Children's Favorites, Vol. 2*. Walt Disney Productions, 1979.

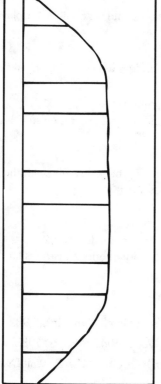

Arch Bridge

Beam Bridge

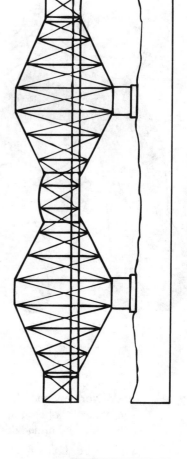

Cantilever Bridge

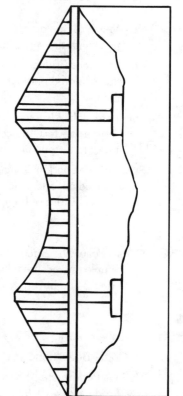

Suspension Bridge

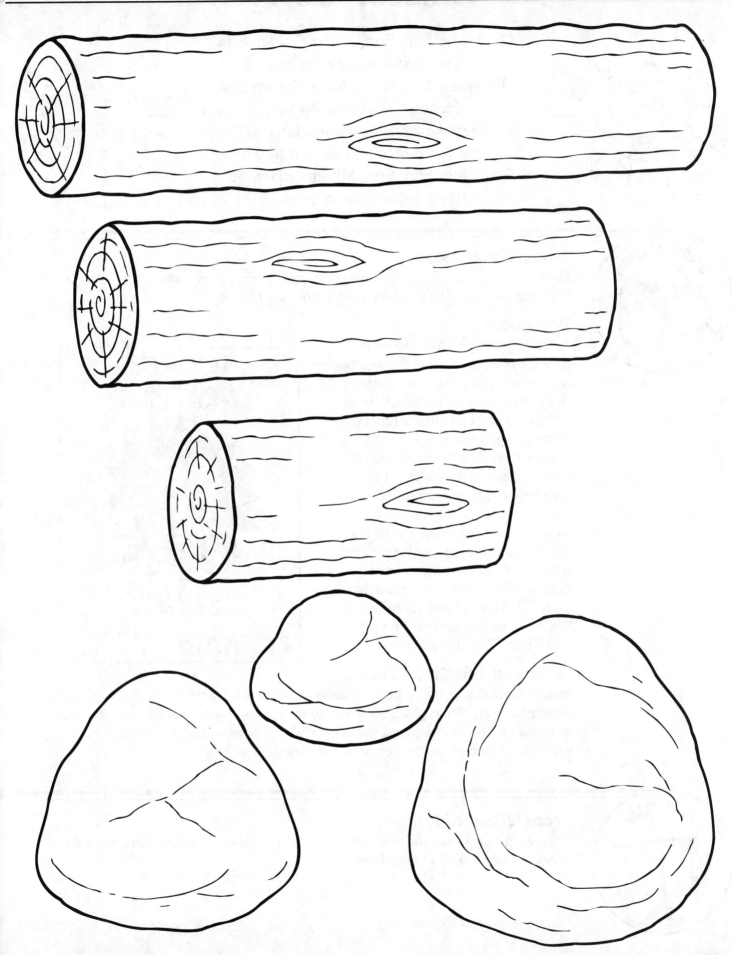

Mister Sun

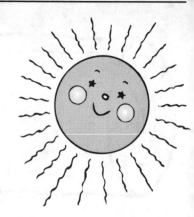

Oh, Mister Sun, Sun, Mister Golden Sun,
Please shine down on me.
Oh, Mister Sun, Sun, Mister Golden Sun,
Please shine down on me.
These little children are asking you
To please come down so we can play in you.
Oh, Mister Sun, Sun, Mister Golden Sun,
Please shine down on me.

Props/Visual Aids
Purchase a weather chart, available commercially from many school suppliers, or make a chart using the patterns provided on page 55.

Talk About
At the beginning of your circle time, have the children observe the weather conditions. Use a window near your circle time area with a view of the sky, or take the children outside (briefly!) so they may also feel any change in temperature. Use the chart and pictures to describe the weather the children have observed. On sunny and partly sunny days, sing the song as written. You can change the words to reflect other types of weather or sing other songs with weather-related themes. On a rainy day you might sing, "Oh, Drippy Rain, Rain, Drippy Wet Rain, please don't drip on me" or sing, "Rain, Rain, Go Away."

TODAY'S WEATHER

SUNNY WARM 65°

To Extend This Circle Time
Invite several children to pretend to experience specific weather conditions. Use the patterns on page 55 to give a silent cue to the actors. As the children act out their responses to the weather, have the other children observe and then guess what weather conditions the children are dramatizing.

Props/Visual Aids
Bring to the classroom the weather page from a local newspaper or videotape the previous night's local weather forecast.

TODAY'S WEATHER

Talk About

Meteorologists use scientific data to predict the weather. Share the predictions with the children. Ask, "Were the predictions right? Is it really raining today?" Have the class make some predictions of their own for the next day's weather. Record them and then compare them to the meteorologists' forecast. The *Old Farmers' Almanac* by Robert B. Thomas is published yearly and available at many discount stores. This book includes weather predictions for the United States for a whole year! Look at the almanac with the children and check the predictions for your region. Are they accurate?

To Extend This Circle Time

Take a field trip to a local television station or invite a meteorologist to visit your classroom. List questions the children would like to ask before the visit or trip. Set up your dramatic play area to represent a television studio. Have the children work in small groups to make weather predictions. Use a camcorder to videotape the children presenting their forecasts and weather reports. Share the tape with parents.

Problem Solving

Props/Visual Aids

Supply a collection of clothing worn in different types of weather. Use real items if possible or cut out pictures of clothing from magazines and catalogs. You will also need chart paper and markers.

Talk About

Vary the words to the song to describe a kind of weather. You might sing, "Mister Snow, Snow, Mister White Bright Snow" and "these little children are asking you, what we should wear so we can play in you." Ask the children, "What should we wear when it is snowing outside?" "What do we need to wear if it is raining?" Record their suggestions on the chart paper.

To Extend This Circle Time

Provide your dramatic play area with a variety of weather-related clothing such as boots, hats, mittens, coats and shorts; and equipment such as umbrellas, shovels and empty sunscreen bottles. Suggest different types of weather situations as they play. "Oh, no! This is a BIG snowstorm! What do we need to wear today?"

Communication

Props/ Visual Aids

Make a classroom chart with four columns. Label the first column with the date and label the next three columns *Yesterday*, *Today* and *Tomorrow*.

Talk About

Ask, "Do you remember what the weather was like yesterday?" Draw a simple representation such as a sun, rain cloud or snowflake in the *Yesterday* column. Discuss the weather conditions for today and ask the children to make a prediction for tomorrow's weather. Record both in the appropriate columns. Do this activity for a selected period of time. Discuss any patterns in the weather. "Last week it rained four days!" "We thought it would be sunny today, and it is."

DATE	YESTERDAY	TODAY	TOMORROW
April 22, 1996			

To Extend This Circle Time

Make sunny day cookies. You will need refrigerated sugar cookie dough (available commercially in tubes), powdered sugar, milk and food coloring. Prepare the cookies according to the package directions. Mix the powdered sugar with a little milk to make a simple frosting. Add food coloring to make the frosting yellow. Have the children use craft sticks or plastic knives to spread the frosting on the cookies to make little suns. Blue frosting could be used to make raindrop cookies and white frosting for snowball cookies. Enjoy the cookies with glasses of cold milk!

Books to Share

Borden, Louise. *Caps, Hats, Socks, and Mittens: A Book About the Four Seasons.* Scholastic, 1989.
> Very simple text and colorful, whimsical drawings describe some of the pleasures, activities and clothing of each season.

DeWitt, Lynda. *What Will the Weather Be?* HarperCollins, 1991.
> Simple text and clear illustrations explain basic characteristics of weather and how meteorologists gather data for their forecasts.

Elliott, Alan. *On Sunday the Wind Came.* William Morrow and Company, 1980.
> Soft, wash illustrations depict a young boy who describes the weather on each day of the week and what he will play with his friends.

Rogers, Paul. *What Will the Weather Be Like Today?* Greenwillow Books, 1989.
> Birds, animals and people discuss the possibilities of the day's weather in simple rhyming verse with cut-paper illustrations.

Weiss, Nicki. *On a Hot, Hot Day.* G.P. Putnam's Sons, 1992.
> A mother and her child can find something fun to do, whether it's cold and wet; snowy; or a hot, hot day.

Willis, Jeanne. *Earth Weather as Explained by Professor Xargle.* Dutton's Children's Books, 1991.
> Professor Xargle explains to his class of extraterrestrials how humans behave in different kinds of weather.

Tapes and CDs

McGrath, Bob. "Mr. Sun" from *Sing Along with Bob, Vol. 1.* Kids' Records, 1984.

Raffi. "Mr. Sun" from *Singable Songs for the Very Young.* Shoreline, 1979.

Roth, Kevin. "Mr. Sun, Sun" from *Dinosaurs, Dragons and Other Children's Songs.* Marlboro Records, Inc., 1990.

Various Performers. "Mr. Sun" from *Car Songs: Songs to Sing Anywhere.* Kimbo, 1990.

The North Wind Doth Blow

The north wind doth blow
And we shall have snow,
And what will poor robin do then?
Poor thing!
He'll sit in the barn
And keep himself warm
And hide his head under his wing.
Poor thing!

Props/Visual Aids

Purchase a small weather vane and place it outside near a classroom window or on your playground. Try to find an area without large trees or buildings which might obstruct the wind. Post the "N," "S," "E" and "W" signs from pages 60 and 61 the appropriate walls in your classroom.

Talk About

Observe the direction from which the wind is blowing as a part of your opening circle time activities. Record the direction on your weather chart. Have the children extend their arms in the direction of the wind, using the N, S, E and W signs as prompts. Ask, "How does the wind feel today?"

To Extend This Circle Time

Invite the children to move around the classroom using the directions N, S, E and W instead of left and right. You might say, "Walk north from the door to the water fountain. Then walk west to our block area."

Props/Visual Aids

You will need two or three balloons, crepe paper, tape, a small oscillating fan, baby powder, bubble solution and wand, a small spray bottle of water and a few paper towels.

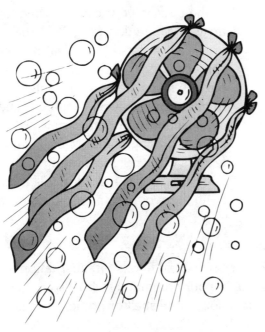

Talk About

There are a number of ways for your children to experience the wind without going outside. Blow up a balloon and release it. Have the children hold up their hands to feel the air moving out of the balloon. Turn on the fan. Sprinkle a small amount of baby powder into the air above the fan. The children will be able to "see" the wind as the fan blows the particles of powder. Attach streamers of crepe paper to the fan or to an open window. Watch as the breeze blows the paper. Blow bubbles or spray water in a fine mist in front of the fan. Ask, "Which direction will the bubbles float? How far will the water blow? What will happen if we make the fan run faster? Slower?"

To Extend This Circle Time

Make simple wind socks with the children. Supply the art center with large pieces of construction paper, washable markers, yarn and 2' (.61 m) lengths of crepe paper streamers. Have each child decorate a piece of construction paper and help him or her roll it into a tube. Secure it with staples or tape. Use a hole punch to make two holes in the tube as shown. Thread a piece of yarn through the holes and tie it. Use tape or staples to attach crepe paper streamers to the other end of the tube to complete the wind sock. Ask, "What will happen if you run while holding your wind sock? How about if you walk slowly?" Hang the wind socks near a window or doorway to watch the air flow move the streamers.

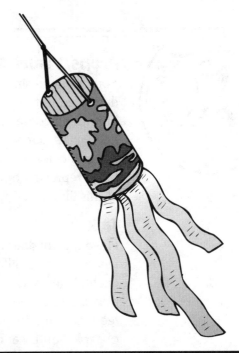

Props/Visual Aids

Gather information from your library on the migratory birds in your area. You might also contact any local bird-watching groups or the National Audubon Society.

Talk About

Poor Robin! Robins usually migrate out of wintry climates. This poor bird will have to sit in a barn to stay warm. Share with your children what happens to the birds in your climate when the winter months arrive. Where do they go? Perhaps you live in an area that winters birds. What new birds arrive in the winter months? Ask, "What can we do to help the birds that stay here in the winter?" Responses might include leaving windbreak shelters in fields, supplying fresh (not frozen) water to drink and, of course, feeding them! Make a variety of simple bird feeders with your class, using plastic two-liter bottles with holes cut in the sides. Fill them with seed and hang them outside near a classroom window.

To Extend This Circle Time

Talk about what other small animals do in the winter months. Ask, "What do squirrels do in winter? Rabbits? Turtles?" Find books on hibernation to share with the children. There may be people in your community who also require extra assistance in the winter months. Contact a local food shelf or homeless shelter to see how your class can help.

Communication

Props/Visual Aids

You will need simple bird feeders as described in the previous circle time or purchased commercially. You will also need chart paper and markers. Cut out and color the bird outlines on page 62 to represent birds seen in your area at this time of year.

Talk About

Have the children help you fill the bird feeders. Use a different kind of seed in each feeder, such as thistle seeds, mixed and sunflower seeds. Hang the feeders where they can easily be observed and scatter some seed on the ground. Watch the feeders for several days and keep track on the chart paper how many and what kinds of birds the children see and what kinds of seeds they eat. How often do you have to refill each feeder? Use the bird cut-outs on the chart to depict the birds you observe.

To Extend This Circle Time

Supply your art area with paper, glue and washable markers or crayons. Invite the children to draw their favorite birds. Help each child decide what seeds his or her bird preferred and glue some of the seeds on the picture. Ask the child to dictate a caption and write it on the bottom. Display the pictures around the room.

Books to Share

Carlstrom, Nancy White. *How Does the Wind Walk?* Macmillan, 1993.
Colorful acrylic paintings accompany this story of a little boy who plays with the wind in each of the four seasons and through all its changing moods.

Ets, Marie Hall. *Gilberto and the Wind*. Viking Press, 1963.
Gilberto plays with the wind, which is sometimes gentle to his balloon, sailboat, pinwheel and bubbles, and sometimes so strong Gilberto hides in his house from the breaking branches of trees.

Kent, Jack. *Round Robin*. Prentice Hall, 1982.
Cartoon-like drawings help tell the humorous story of a robin who has eaten until he looks more like a ball than a bird and discovers when fall comes that he can only hop south while the other robins fly.

Lipson, Michael. *How the Wind Plays*. Hyperion Books for Children, 1994.
The wind, pictured as a mischievous child, shakes branches against the window, pushes snow under the windowsill and sighs as it wonders what game to play next.

Rockwell, Anne. *Our Yard Is Full of Birds*. Macmillan, 1992.
Accurate paintings help tell the story of a little boy and the birds he likes to watch through all the seasons of the year, including swallows, mourning doves, chickadees and jays.

Ryder, Joanne. *Catching the Wind*. Morrow Junior Books, 1989.
Called by the wind, a child is transformed into a bird for a day and joins a flock of geese in a glorious flight.

Resources

Kaufman, John. *Robins Fly North, Robins Fly South*. Thomas Y. Crowell Company, 1970.
This story of robin migration has accurate detailed drawings and depicts the birds' preparation for flight, travel and establishment of territories that provide food and protection for their families.

Oram, Liz. *Bird Migration*. Steck-Vaughn, 1992.
Photographs and maps help discuss the migration patterns of such birds as sparrows, owls, chickadees, robins, swallows and penguins.

Tapes and CDs

Ambrosian Children's Choir. "The North Wind Doth Blow" from *Sing Children Sing: Songs of the British Isles*. Caedmon, 1979.

Barolk Folk with Madeline MacNeil and Barbara Hess. "The North Wind Doth Blow" from *Girls and Boys Come Out to Play*. Music for Little People, 1991.

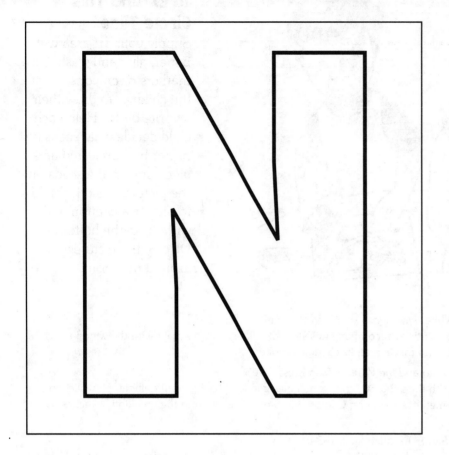

60

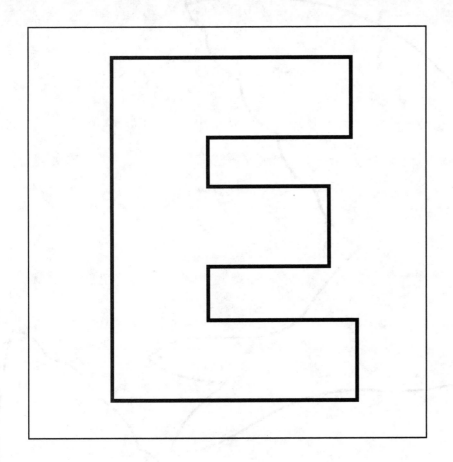

Open Them, Shut Them

Open them, shut them,
Open them, shut them,
Give a little clap.
Open them, shut them,
Open them, shut them,
Lay them in your lap.

Creep them, creep them,
Way up to your chin.
Open up your mouth,
But do not let them in!

Open them, shut them,
Open them, shut them,
To your shoulders fly.
Then like little birdies,
Let them flutter to the sky.

Falling, falling, to the ground,
Pick them up again and
Turn them round and round.
Faster, faster, slower now.
(repeat first verse)

Props/Visual Aids

You will need chart paper and markers. You may choose to use an instant camera or camcorder. Give each child two sheets of paper, one labeled *Open* and the other *Shut* and several crayons or washable markers.

Talk About

Say, "Many parts of our bodies can open and shut. What are some things that you can open and shut?" List the children's ideas on chart paper, using simple illustrations if possible. Sing the first verse of the song, opening and shutting different parts of your body. Take a photograph or video of each child with his or her face open and shut. Have the children compare the images and draw how their faces look.

To Extend This Circle Time

Ask, "What other things in our classroom open and shut?" Some answers might include scissors, curtains, cupboards, drawers, containers with lids and markers with caps. Divide the children into pairs. Invite them to move around the classroom, discovering objects that open and shut. One child in the pair can open the object and the other child shut it.

Prediction

Props/Visual Aids

You will need large plastic tweezers, such as the type found in many toy doctor or nurse kits, dry beans and small plastic containers.

Talk About

Allow the children to practice using the tweezers and then invite them to play a prediction game. Have the children take turns sitting in a chair in the center of the circle. Place a plastic container on the floor at their feet. Using the plastic tweezers, have the children pick up beans from another container and try to drop them into the container on the floor. Ask, "How many do you think you will drop into the bucket? How many really went in?" Give each child five beans on the first turn and 10 beans the second time.

To Extend This Circle Time

Bring a variety of containers with different kinds of lids. Have the children practice opening and shutting the containers. Allow them to continue practicing with the tweezers and to use them to fill the containers with beans.

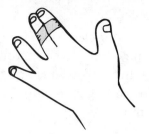

Props/Visual Aids

With masking tape, fasten together different combinations of the children's adjacent fingers. (Be sure the tape is not tight enough to interfere with blood circulation.) On some children, tape together the pinky and ring fingers, on others the pointer and middle fingers, or the thumb and pointer. Provide a variety of sizes of beads and two plastic containers for each child.

Talk About

Have the children work with their fingers to move their beads from one container to the other. If the containers have lids, have the children try to remove or fasten the lids. Ask the children questions to help them describe the level of difficulty or the amount of frustration they are experiencing. What are they doing to help make the task easier? As the children gain skill, tape additional fingers together. Have the children play in the classroom or try to complete other tasks with their fingers taped.

To Extend This Circle Time

Humans are one of the few animals with opposable thumbs. Thumbs enable us to open, shut and manipulate our hands to perform a variety of intricate tasks. Collect, display and discuss pictures of animals with and without thumbs.

Props/Visual Aids

Share with the class a book or video on sign language. See "Books to Share" for several wonderful titles.

Talk About

People who are hearing impaired may use sign language to communicate. Invite a parent or teacher who knows sign language to visit your class and teach the children some simple signs. Incorporate them into your daily routines. See page 67 for some common signs and their meanings.

To Extend This Circle Time

Create some new sign language signs for your classroom using different hand motions or facial expressions. Use the new signs to communicate classroom transitions. Ask the children for ideas and list the movements and their meanings on a chart. You might have two winks and three fingers mean "it is time to pick up" or a smile and tummy rub mean "it's snack time."

Books to Share

Ancona, George. *Handtalk Zoo*. Four Winds Press, 1989.
Words and bright photographs of children using sign language tell of a trip to the zoo where the children discover how to sign the names of various animals and to tell time.

Bornstein, Harry. *Nursery Rhymes from Mother Goose Told in Signed English*. Kendall Green Productions, 1993.
Familiar Mother Goose rhymes are accompanied by simple diagrams showing how to form the Signed English signs for each word in the poems.

Charlip, Remy. *Handtalk: An ABC of Finger Spelling and Sign Language*. Parents' Magazine Press, 1974.
Photographs introduce two kinds of sign language: finger spelling, or forming words letter by letter with the fingers; and signing, or making signs with one or two hands for each word or idea.

Charlip, Remy. *Handtalk Birthday: A Number and Story Book in Sign Language*. Four Winds Press, 1987.
Clear photographs of signing and words depict friends helping a deaf woman celebrate her birthday with presents, cake and a special wish come true.

Fain, Kathleen. *Handsigns: A Sign Language Alphabet*. Chronicle Books, 1993.
Colorful pictures present an animal for each letter of the alphabet accompanied by the corresponding sign for that letter in American Sign Language.

Rankin, Laura. *The Handmade Alphabet*. Dial Books, 1991.
Beautiful colored pencil drawings depict hands signing each letter of the manual alphabet used in American Sign Language.

Yabuuchi, Masayuki. *Whose Footprints?* Philomel Books, 1985.
Accurate paintings and very simple text depict the footprints of a monkey, duck, cat, horse, hippopotamus, bear and goat.

Tapes and CDs

Hammett, Carol. "Open, Shut Them" from *Preschool Action Time*. Kimbo, 1988.

Monet, Lisa. "Open/Shut Them" from *Circle Time: Songs and Rhymes for the Very Young*. Monet Productions, 1986.

I   Am   Hungry

Peanut   Butter   Jelly   Sandwich

Please   Thank You   Love

Yellow   Red   Blue   Green

Peanut Butter and Jelly

(chorus)
Peanut, peanut butter, jelly.
Peanut, peanut butter, jelly.

(verses)
First, you have to pick it, you pick it,
you pick it, pick it, pick it.
Then you crack it, you crack it,
you crack it, crack it, crack it.
Then you mash it, you mash it,
you mash it, mash it, mash it.

(sing chorus twice)
Then you stir it, you stir it,
you stir it, stir it, stir it.
Then you spread it, you spread it,
you spread it, spread it, spread it.
Then you eat it, you eat it,
you eat it, eat it, eat it.

(sing chorus twice)
Then you chew it, you chew it,
you chew it, chew it, chew it.

(Sing chorus twice as if your mouth is stuck with peanut butter.)

Props/Visual Aids

You will need several kinds of peanut butter such as chunky, creamy, different store brands or homemade. You can also do this activity with different kinds of jelly such as strawberry, grape and apple. Give each child a small paper plate and a craft stick. Record the children's responses on chart paper. Be aware of any children that have food allergies before you begin.

Talk About

Give each child a small amount of each type of peanut butter or jelly. (Don't do peanut butter and jelly at the same time.) Depending on the age of your children, you may choose to give just one sample at a time. Tell the children you are going to look at, smell and touch the peanut butter (or jelly). Ask the children to smell the samples. "Careful, don't get any on your nose! Which smells the most like peanuts? Which jelly smells most like the fruit?" Record the children's comments on the chart paper.

Have the children touch the peanut butter or jelly. Ask, "How does it feel? Does it feel smooth or lumpy? Can you feel any peanuts or seeds?" Record their responses. Have the children use their craft sticks to spread the peanut butter or jelly on the paper plate. Which is the easiest to spread? Which was the stickiest?

To Extend This Circle Time

The words in the song give directions to make a peanut butter and jelly sandwich. What might the words be to make a different kind of sandwich? Have the class select another type of sandwich to make. Provide the ingredients and demonstrate the preparation as the children identify the steps involved. Use those steps to write words for a new song.

You might sing these words for "The Egg Salad Song":

(chorus)   Eggs and bread and mayo, mayo
                Eggs and bread and mayo, mayo.

(verses) 1. First you take the eggs and you boil them, you boil them.
             Bubble, bubble, bubble, boil them.
         2. Then you peel them . . .
         3. Then you smash them . . .
         4. Then you add the mayo . . .
         5. Then you mix them . . .

Props/Visual Aids

Supply four different kinds each of peanut butter, jelly and bread. You might have creamy, chunky, low fat and homemade peanut butter; and grape, apple and strawberry jelly; and honey. Honey is not a jelly, of course, but it is a delicious spread with peanut butter! For the breads, you might choose white, whole wheat, English muffins and graham crackers. Make a copy of the prediction page on page 72 for each of the four types of ingredients. The left section of the page will be used to predict the children's preferences, and the right section to record likes and dislikes after a taste test. At the top of the chart write the name and draw a simple representation of the type of ingredient you will be testing.

Talk About

Ask the children to remember the best peanut butter and jelly sandwich they ever ate. Describe in detail the most delicious peanut butter sandwich you ever had. Say, "We are going to figure out how to make the very best sandwich!" Follow these steps for each ingredient: First, show the children one kind of peanut butter. Pass it around the group and ask each child if he or she thinks it would taste good or bad in the sandwich or if he or she doesn't know. Record the responses on the Prediction Page by writing the child's name under the face depicting his or her response. Count the number of children listed under each prediction. Then give each child a taste of the peanut butter, and record his or her reaction on the right section of the page. Compare the two sets of responses. Did anyone change his or her mind? Why?

Problem Solving

Props/Visual Aids

Peanut Butter

1 bag of peanuts in the shell peanut oil
salt   blender

Open the bag of peanuts and have the children shell them and remove the skins. Taste the peanuts. Ask, "Does this taste like peanut butter? What do you think we need to do?" Put the peanuts in the blender and blend until smooth. Add a few teaspoons of peanut oil and salt to taste.

No Cook Jam

3 cups (720 ml) mashed fruit   5 cups (1200 ml) sugar (amount
1 package of pectin   may vary depending on the
3/4 cup (180 ml) boiling water   type of fruit)
freezer   small jars with lids

Mix the mashed fruit and sugar and allow to sit for 20 minutes, until the sugar dissolves. Dissolve one package of pectin in 3/4 cup (180 ml) of water. Boil together for one minute. Pour onto the fruit mixture and stir for three minutes. Put in jars and close the lids tightly. Let the jelly stand for 24 hours. Freeze unused jars until you are ready to use them.

To Extend This Circle Time

Arrange all the ingredients in your snack area. Allow the children to assemble their own sandwiches. "Whose sandwich do you think will be the best?" Eat and enjoy!

Talk About

Decide with your class whether to make peanut butter or jelly. If you choose to do both, enlist extra adults to help and divide your class into two groups, each group making one of the recipes. Say, "Today we are going to make peanut butter and jelly sandwiches, but we have a BIG problem! We don't have any peanut butter and jelly, so we have to make it!" Have the children wash their hands. Be aware if any children have food allergies before beginnng.

As you prepare the recipes, ask the children questions such as "What do you think we need to do next? What will happen when . . . ?" Use the finished peanut butter and jelly to make some great sandwiches!

Props/Visual Aids

Make peanut butter and jelly sandwiches using a variety of spreads and bread. Cut the sandwiches into bite-size pieces so that each child may have a taste. Reproduce the "We Like _____ Best" page on page 73, making one copy for each type of sandwich.

Talk About

Show the children each type of sandwich and describe the ingredients. Remind them of the types of ingredients they may have sampled in previous circle times. Give each child a taste of one type of sandwich. Complete a "We Like _____ Best" page for that sandwich with the children's comments. You might write, "Jimmy likes creamy peanut butter because it is not lumpy" or "Min thinks strawberry jam is sweet."

To Extend This Circle Time

Bind the "We Like _____ Best" pages together to make a class book. Share the book with parents.

Books to Share

Blos, Joan W. *The Hungry Little Boy.* Simon & Schuster Books for Young Readers, 1995.
   Bright oil paintings help tell the story of a young boy's peanut butter sandwich lunch that his grandmother has carefully prepared.

Joosse, Barbara, M. *Jam Day.* Harper & Row, 1987.
   An annual family reunion involving berry picking and jam making reminds Ben that he is part of a big, noisy family.

Mahy, Margaret. *Jam: A True Story.* Atlantic Monthly Press, 1985.
   When Mr. Castle stays home with the three little Castles, he also makes pots and pots of plum jam, until every jar and vase are filled and they have too much of a good thing.

Peters, Lisa Westberg. *Purple Delicious Blackberry Jam.* Arcade Publishing, 1992.
   Freddy and older sister Muff persuade Grandma to make blackberry jam which begins a juicy, prickly, messy, bubbly adventure with a surprise ending.

Robbins, Ken. *Make Me a Peanut Butter Sandwich and a Glass of Milk.* Scholastic, 1992.
   Simple text and hand-tinted photographs show how each part of a peanut butter sandwich and milk for lunch is made, from field, to store, to table.

Westcott, Nadine Bernard. *Peanut Butter and Jelly: A Play Rhyme.* Dutton's Children's Books, 1987.
   Rhyming text and humorous illustrations explain how to make a very large peanut butter and jelly sandwich.

Tapes and CDs

Lehman, Peg. "Peanut Butter & Jelly" from *Critters in the Choir.* Pal Music, 1989.

Sharon, Lois and Bram. "Peanut Butter" from *Smorgasbord.* Elephant Records, 1979.

Sharon, Lois and Bram. "Peanut Butter and Jelly" from *Great Big Hits.* A&M Records, 1992.

Prediction for

_____

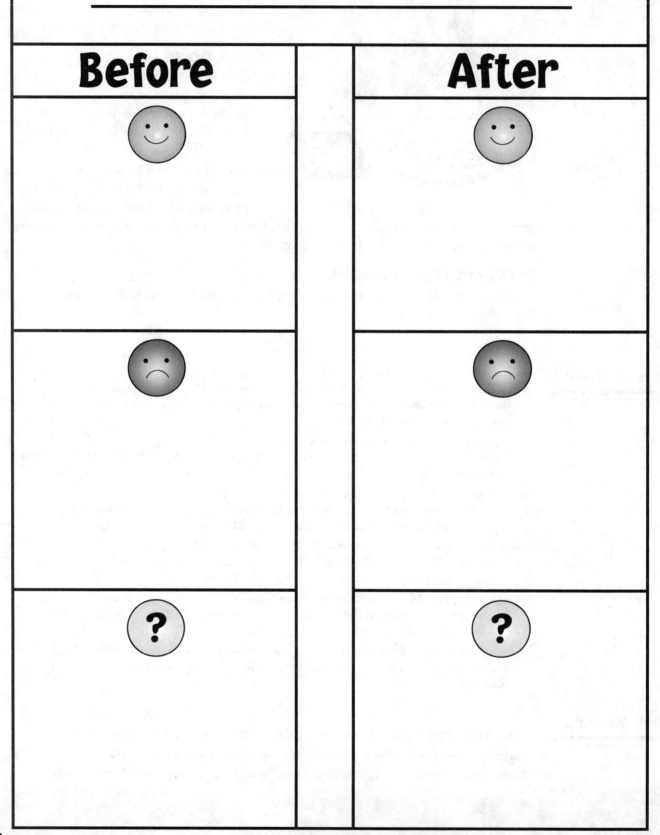

Before	After
🙂	🙂
🙁	🙁
?	?

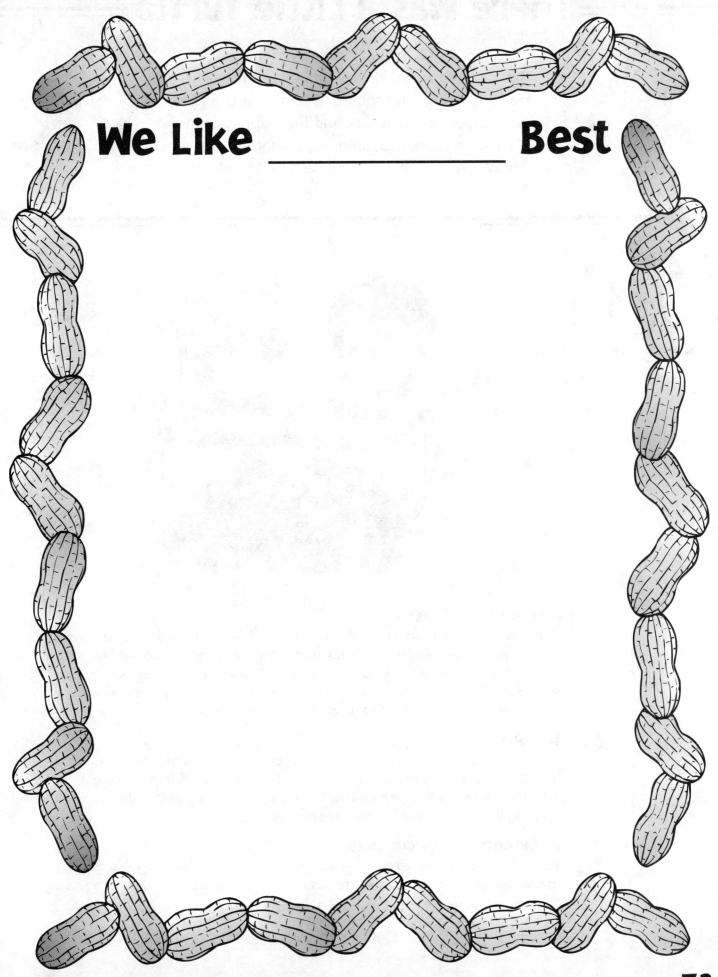

We Like _____ Best

There Was a Little Turtle

There was a little turtle, he lived in a box.
He swam in a puddle, he climbed on the rocks.
He snapped at a mosquito, he snapped at a flea,
He snapped at a minnow, and he snapped at me!
He caught the mosquito, he caught the flea,
He caught the minnow, but he didn't catch me!

Props/Visual Aids

Consider acquiring a turtle for a classroom pet. They are fairly easy to care for, and children enjoy observing them. Some turtles may carry disease, so it is best to not allow the children to hold or touch the turtle. Always wash your hands with soap and water after feeding the turtle or cleaning its tank. A pet store will help you determine the proper size tank and other necessary equipment.

Talk About

Share with the children a variety of books about turtles. Observe the turtle in the tank after allowing it a few days to adjust to classroom life. "What does the turtle eat? How does it eat? Is it a male or female turtle? Does it play in the water and climb on the rocks? Does it have a special name?"

To Extend This Circle Time

Take a field trip to a pet store to see more turtles, or if you live in a fairly rural area near a lake or pond, you may see turtles outside. Remind the children to not touch the turtles or to destroy their natural habitat.

Props/Visual Aids

You will need small balls, or other small items that will float, and large plastic tweezers, such as the type found in many toy doctor or nurse kits. Fill your sensory table with water or use several large dishpans. Be sure to have towels nearby.

Talk About

Say, "This turtle was very hungry! He snapped at mosquitoes, minnows and fleas! He caught them all, too. Do you think you could catch a minnow?" Divide the children into groups. Invite them to take turns pretending they are turtles trying to catch the minnows (floating balls or other objects) with the plastic tweezers. Ask, "How many minnows do you think you will catch?" Record each child's prediction. Give each child a set amount of time to "catch" as many balls as possible. Record the actual number the child caught and then compare it to the prediction.

To Extend This Circle Time

Make turtles from paper bowls and green construction paper. You will also need safety scissors, glue, washable markers or paint and scraps of colored paper. From the green construction paper, help each child cut five oval shapes, making one a little larger than the other four. Glue the larger shape on the rim of the bowl for the head and the remaining ovals for legs. Cut and glue a triangle for the turtle's tail. Turn the bowls upside down and invite the children to decorate their turtles' shells with paint, markers or pieces of colored paper.

Props/Visual Aids

Bring several books with pictures of animals, or use the patterns on pages 78 and 79. Reproduce the turtle without a shell drawing on page 80, making one copy for each child. You will also need several crayons or washable markers for each child.

Talk About

Share the pictures of animals with the children. Discuss different ways the animals protect themselves from danger. Some responses might be:

    rabbit–runs fast
    skunk–smells bad
    squirrel–climbs trees
    porcupine–throws barbed bristles
    cat–has sharp claws and teeth
    opossum–plays dead
    bird–flies away
    mouse–hides in a hole

Say, "The turtle uses its shell for protection. If the turtle didn't have a shell, what do you think the turtle should have to protect itself? How would that help?" Give each child the drawing of the turtle without a shell on page 80 and several crayons. Ask him or her to add something to the turtle to help it protect itself.

To Extend This Circle Time

Make turtle shells for the children to "wear" and hide in. You will need several large boxes, washable paint and medium-sized paintbrushes. In each box, cut out a large area in one end for a child's head. Then cut out an area on each side for arms and two more on the other end for legs. Do not cut holes in the box that may trap a child's head; cut arch-shaped areas that extend to the floor. Invite the children to paint the boxes to look like turtle shells. Have them take turns being turtles and other predator animals. Turtles can pull in their heads and legs and be safe inside their shells.

Props/Visual Aids

There are many wonderful, age-appropriate books about reptiles in your local or school library. Ask your librarian for suggestions.

Talk About

Share pictures of different reptiles. Say, "Turtles are reptiles and are related to lots of other animals. These animals are reptiles, too. How do they look alike? Do you think they eat the same foods? Where do they live?" Have the children help write new words to the fingerplay about another reptile. You might say:

    There was a little snake; she lived in the grass.
    She wriggled in the weeds and she hid when I walked past.

76

To Extend This Circle Time

Create a reptile exhibit in your science area. Invite the children to bring to the classroom their model reptiles–including dinosaurs! Make labels for the types of reptiles and display them with books and other resources. Which kind of reptile is the most popular?

Books to Share

Chermayeff, Ivan. *Scaly Facts.* Harcourt Brace, 1995.
Colorful collages illustrate simple facts about alligators, snakes, turtles, geckoes and other reptiles.

Florian, Douglas. *Turtle Day.* Thomas Y. Crowell, 1989.
Child-like drawings illustrate the very simple text as turtle is busy sunning, swimming and playing all day.

Fowler, Allan. *Turtles Take Their Time.* Children's Press, 1992.
Bright photographs illustrate simple descriptions of the physical characteristics and behavior of turtles.

George, William T. *Box Turtle at Long Pond.* Greenwillow Books, 1989.
Realistic full-page paintings and lyrical writing tell of a box turtle's busy day at Long Pond, searching for food, basking in the sun and escaping a raccoon.

Kuhn, Dwight. *Turtle's Day.* Cobblehill Books, 1994.
Simple text and large colorful photographs follow an eastern box turtle through her day.

Turner, Charles. *The Turtle and the Moon.* Dutton's Children's Books, 1991.
Luminous pastels illustrate this story of a lonely turtle who makes friends with the moon.

Resources

Frisch, Carlienne. *Responsible Pet Care: Turtles.* Rourke Publications, 1991.
Straightforward information on choosing a turtle for a pet and instructions for caring for it.

Vrbova, Zuza. *Junior Pet Care: Turtles.* T.F.H. Publications, Inc., 1990.
Covers all aspects of choosing, buying and caring for turtles as well as information on the nature of turtles.

Twinkle, Twinkle, Little Star

Twinkle, twinkle, little star,
How I wonder what you are.
Up above the world so high,
Like a diamond in the sky.
Twinkle, twinkle, little star,
How I wonder what you are.

Props/Visual Aids

Visit your local library to find books with maps of the stars. They will show the positions of stars in the sky as they appear in your latitude each month of the year. The *Old Farmers' Almanac* also has information on which stars are visible each month.

Talk About

Since most of us go to school during the day, and, of course, viewing stars is easiest at night, you will need to involve parents in some of your star-watching activities. Share pictures of stars. Ask, "Have you ever gone out to look at the stars at night? What did you see? How many stars can you count?"

To Extend This Circle Time

Plan a family field trip one night during the week. Invite parents and children to visit a field, away from any city light pollution. Bring blankets to spread on the ground and hot chocolate in thermoses. Watch the stars in the night sky. Try to identify the constellations you may have shown the children in books. A note of caution: Remind parents to keep close watch on their children so no one is lost or hurt in the dark. Strive for a one-to-one ratio of adults and children. Do not allow children to come on the trip unless accompanied by a parent or other responsible adult.

Prediction

Props/Visual Aids

Ask each child to bring a flashlight from home. A variety of sizes will create differences in the brightness of the "stars." Use reflective paper or tinfoil to cut out a number of circles in different sizes. Attach the circles to the ceiling in your classroom or another room that can be darkened.

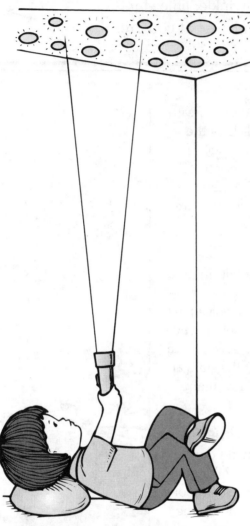

Talk About

Stars do not really have five points. Most of them are round, just like the sun and Earth. It is the distortion of their light, traveling through all of the particles in the atmosphere, that makes them appear to have points and to twinkle. Larger, brighter stars are closer to the Earth than the dimmer, smaller stars. Invite the children, holding their flashlights, to lie on their backs on the carpet. Darken the room. If you have a dimmer switch, use it to give the illusion of dusk deepening to darkness. Shine the flashlights on the ceiling to see the foil reflecting back as "stars." Ask, "Which stars are brightest? Which are dim? What will happen if we shine all of our lights on one star?"

To Extend This Circle Time

Provide your art center with construction paper, tape, glue, glitter and safety scissors. Make copies of the star patterns on page 85. Help the children design and make star headbands. Invite the children to wear their headbands and move about the classroom as stars. Form them into groups or simple constellations. Have them slowly rotate around the classroom just as the stars rotate through the night sky.

Problem Solving

Props/Visual Aids

You will need chart paper and markers.

Talk About

Jane Taylor's original poem "The Star" contains the lines:

"When the blazing sun is gone,
When he nothing shines upon,
Then you show your little light,
Twinkle, twinkle all the night.
Then the traveller in the dark,
Thanks you for your tiny spark;
He could not see which way to go,
If you did not twinkle so."

82

Sing these lesser-known verses with the children. Say, "The traveller in the song could see which way to go because of the shining stars. What if it was a cloudy night and the stars weren't out? How could the traveller see without stars? What could he use to help him see?" List the children's responses on chart paper. You might have, "Use a flashlight, wait until the sun comes up, go where there are streetlights, drive a car with headlights."

To Extend This Circle Time

Make star splatter paintings with the children. Provide black paper, white paint and a plastic drinking straw for each child. Practice blowing through the straws before you begin. Then have each child dip the end of the straw in the paint and blow the paint onto the paper. The paint will splatter into star-like patterns.

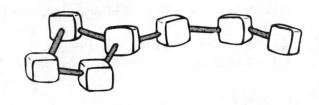

Props/Visual Aids

Use the star map on page 86 to make simple outlines on chart paper of some easily found constellations. Use your library sources to read and explain how those constellations were named.

Talk About

It is often difficult for children (and adults!) to find the picture in a constellation. Telling the story of the constellation will help; most of these myths are exciting and memorable. Show the children the drawing on chart paper of the stars in the constellation. Connect the stars to see the picture. You may want to practice drawing the more difficult constellations before class. Then on another paper, ask the children to help you connect the stars in a new way. Ask, "What other pictures can you see in the stars? Can we make up a new story for this picture?"

To Extend This Circle Time

Have the children make constellations they can eat! You will need miniature marshmallows and pretzel sticks. Give each child 10 of each. Have the children connect the marshmallow "stars" with the pretzels. Can they make some constellation shapes? Invite them to tell stories about the constellations they have created. Then enjoy the snack!

Books to Share

Gibbons, Gail. *Stargazers*. Holiday House, 1992.
Clear, vibrant illustrations and simple text explains what stars are, why they twinkle, how constellations were named, how telescopes are used to study stars and more.

Hines, Anna Grossnickle. *Sky All Around*. Clarion Books, 1989.
A father and daughter share a special time, looking at stars and naming constellations under a crescent moon.

Ichikawa, Satomi. *Nora's Stars*. Philomel Books, 1989.
While visiting her grandmother, Nora and the animated toys from an old chest bring the stars down from the night sky, but their loss makes the sky dark and sad.

Ray, Deborah Kogan. *Stargazing Sky*. Crown Publishers, 1991.
A little girl and her mother stay up late to watch the starry night sky and see a shower of shooting stars.

Spohn, Kate. *Night Goes By*. Macmillan Books for Young Readers, 1995.
Cheerful paintings illustrate this simple story of Sun, Moon and Star visiting one another and taking turns shining in the sky.

Stone, Kazuko G. *Good Night, Twinklegator*. Scholastic, Inc., 1990.
Alligay plays connect the dots with the stars to make Twinklegator, an imaginary friend, who comes down to play.

Taylor, Harriet Peck. *Coyote Places the Stars*. Bradbury Press, 1993.
Based on a Wasco Indian legend, this story tells of Coyote, who arranges the stars in the shapes of his animal friends.

Wright, Kit. *Tigerella*. Scholastic, 1992.
Whimsical illustrations and verse tell the story of Ella who is well-behaved during the day but becomes Tigerella at night and frolics among the stars and constellations.

Resources

Berger, Melvin. *Star Gazing, Comet Tracking and Sky Mapping*. G.P. Putnam's Sons, 1985.
Explains how to learn about stars, constellations, comets and other astronomical phenomena by studying the sky without a telescope.

Levitt, I. M., and Roy K. Marshall. *Star Maps for Beginners*. Simon & Schuster Fireside Books, 1992.
Includes 12 maps, one for each month, showing the positions of the constellations, history and ancient legends about them, tables that give the positions of the planets, an overview of the solar system and more.

Tapes and CDs

McGrath, Bob. "Twinkle, Twinkle, Little Star" from *Sing Along with Bob, Vol. 2*. Kids' Records, 1985.

Raffi. "Twinkle, Twinkle, Little Star" from *One Light, One Sun*. Troubadour Records, 1985.

Sharon, Lois and Bram. "Twinkle, Twinkle, Little Star" from *One Elephant, Deux Elephants*. Elephant Records, 1980.

Various Performers. "Twinkle, Twinkle, Little Star" from *Car Songs: Songs to Sing Anywhere*. Kimbo, 1990.

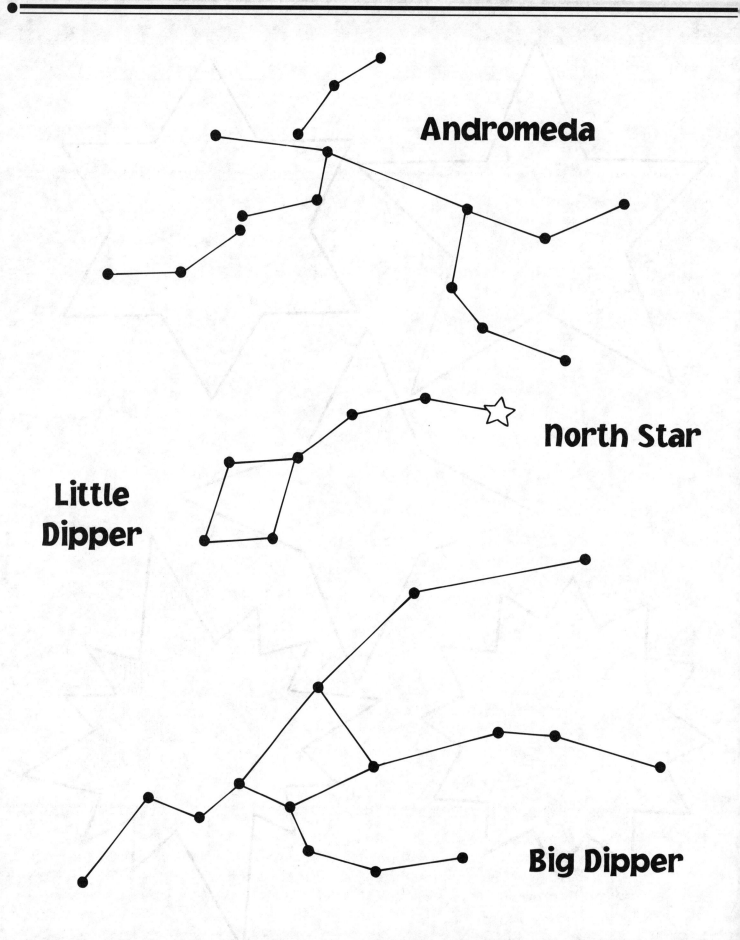

Andromeda

North Star

Little Dipper

Big Dipper

Two Little Apples

Two little apples, hanging on a tree.
Two little apples, smiling at me.
I shook that tree as hard as I could.
Down came the apples.
Mmm! They were good!

Props/Visual Aids

Bring to the circle time a variety of apples. Choose as many different sizes, colors and shapes as possible. Try to have enough apples so that each child may have one.

Talk About

Apples vary by size, color, taste, texture and smell. Give each child an apple to hold and ask them to look at it carefully. Ask, "Is your apple the same color all over, or does it have different colors? Does it have a stem? Is it hard or soft? How does it smell?" Ask the children to place their apples in a basket. Pass the basket around the class. Can each child find his or her own apple? Ask, "How can you tell this apple is yours?"

To Extend This Circle Time

Make apple prints. You will need washable paint, shallow trays or plates, paper towels, paper, apples and a sharp knife. Cut the different varieties of apples in half, some lengthwise through the blossom end and stem and others horizontally through the middle. Place the paint in trays, using a few paper towels as an ink pad. Have the children dip the apple halves into the paint and stamp designs on their papers. How do the apple prints differ?

Props/Visual Aids

You will need three apples of varying sizes–small, medium and large; a sharp knife and a small paper cup for each apple. Reproduce the apple chart on page 90. Make one for each child or enlarge one for the whole group, depending on the skill level of your class.

Talk About

Ask, "How many seeds do you think are in an apple? Do you think a big apple will have more seeds than a small apple?" Pass around the small apple. Have the children look at it carefully and predict the number of seeds inside. Record the prediction on the chart. Repeat for the medium and large apples. Cut open each apple and carefully find and count the seeds. Put the seeds in the cups and record the numbers on the chart. Ask, "Are the numbers the same? Were our predictions right?"

To Extend This Circle Time

Make apple juice. Borrow an apple press or juicer. Have the children help feed the apples into the press. Ask, "What do you think will happen when the apple is pressed? What will be left when the apple juice is squeezed out?" Let the children examine the pulp. Enjoy the juice with your snack!

Props/Visual Aids

Reproduce the patterns on pages 91 and 92. Color, cut out and prepare for use on the flannel board. You will also need chart paper and markers.

Talk About

Say, "In the rhyme, there were two apples in a tree and the child couldn't reach them. What did she do to get the apples? What if she shook the tree and nothing happened? How else could she have gotten the apples?" Record the children's ideas on the chart paper. When possible, illustrate their ideas with the patterns, or place one of the patterns on the flannel board with the apples, tree and child. Ask, "How might a squirrel help the child get the apples? Can you think of a way the ball might help? The ladder?" Allow the children to manipulate the pieces as they help the child get the apples.

To Extend This Circle Time

Make smiling apple pancakes. Add cooked, peeled and chopped apple and a little cinnamon to pancake batter. Make small pancakes so that each child may have two. Use canned whipped topping to decorate the pancakes with smiling faces.

Communication

Props/Visual Aids
Bring to the circle time a variety of apples, a knife and small plates or napkins. Cut out large apple shapes from chart paper, one for each variety of apple.

Talk About
Write the type of each apple on a chart paper shape. Have the children taste one variety of apple. Discuss the apple's flavor and texture. Ask, "How does this kind of apple taste? Is it sour? Sweet? Do you like it?" Record the children's responses on the chart paper for each type of apple. Then have the children rate each apple using a system of one to four stars.

To Extend This Circle Time
Apples are used to make many different types of food. Bring in a variety of foods made with apples for the children to sample. You might have applesauce, apple butter, apple jelly, dried apples, apple pie filling, apple juice. Which do the children like best? Which tastes the most like fresh apples? Have the children rate the apple foods with the system of one to four stars.

Books to Share

Lindbergh, Reeve. *Johnny Appleseed*. Little, Brown and Company, 1990.
Rhymed text and lively, folk art paintings relate the life of John Chapman, whose distribution of apple seed and trees across the Midwest made him a legend.

Maestro, Betsy. *How Do Apples Grow?* HarperCollins, 1992.
Simple text and detailed illustrations describe the life cycle of an apple, from a spring bud to flower to fruit.

Slawson, Michele Benoit. *Apple Picking Time*. Crown Publishers, Inc., 1994.
A young girl, her family and others from their small town all work together to harvest apples when it is apple picking time.

Tryon, Leslie. *Albert's Field Trip*. Atheneum, 1993.
Albert leads a class on a memorable field trip to an apple farm where they pick apples, watch apples being squeezed into juice and eat apple pies.

How Many Seeds?

Size of Apple	We Predicted	We Found

Where Is Thumbkin?

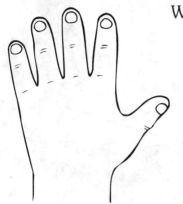
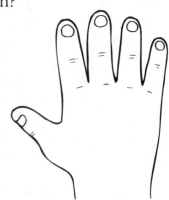

Where is Thumbkin? Where is Thumbkin?
Here I am. Here I am.
How are you today, sir?
Very well, I thank you.
Run away. Run away.

(additional verses)

Where is Pointer?
Where is Middleman?
Where is Ringer?
Where is Pinky?

Props/Visual Aids

Use an instant camera to take a close-up photograph of each child's right or left hand. You may want to secretly code the pictures to help identify them later.

Talk About

Give each child the photograph of his or her hand. As you sing the song, have the children hold up their photographs and point to the correct finger. Put the photographs all together and mix them up. Have the children carefully examine their own hands and compare them to the photos. Can they find the picture that matches their hand?

To Extend This Circle Time

Provide your art center with washable ink pads, paper, warm water and paper towels. Help the children make handprints on the paper. Compare the prints to their hands. Can they identify which prints belong to them? For another observation activity to do at home, help the children make prints of their feet. The children can compare these footprints to the prints made on their birth certificates. Are they similar? How have they changed?

Props/Visual Aids

Trace around each child's hand and cut out the tracing. Make and cut out a separate tracing of each child's thumb. Label the hand and thumb cut-outs with the child's name.

Talk About

Long ago, distances and things were measured by the length of a person's hand or foot. Today, horses are still measured in "hands" which are units of 4" (10 cm). Have the children use their hand and thumb cut-outs to measure distances or items in the room. Ask them to predict how many hands long the sensory table is, how many hands tall the mirror is or how many thumbs wide the door is.

To Extend This Circle Time

Ask the children to make hand tracings of other family members. How many of Dad's hands will it take to measure the kitchen table? How many of the baby's?

Props/Visual Aids

Use the hand and thumb tracings you made for each child in the Prediction Circle Time.

Talk About

Show the children 12" (30 cm) rulers and yardsticks (metersticks). Measure their hand and thumb tracings with the rulers. How long are they? Move around the room and measure the items whose lengths were predicted in the previous circle time. Use both the rulers and the hand and thumb tracings to measure.

To Extend This Circle Time

Create a "How Tall Are We?" chart. See page 96. Write each child's name on the chart and measure the child in hand and thumb tracings and in inches (centimeters). Record the measurements on the chart.

Props/Visual Aids

Use tagboard to make charts with four columns. Draw a simple illustration above each column: names of the children (a smiling face), measurement in inches (centimeters) (ruler), measurement in hands (hand outline) and measurement in thumb lengths (thumb outline).

DOOR

😊	📏	🖐	👍
Jimmy	30 in.	7½	20
Vanessa	30 in.	8	21
Juanita	30 in.	8	22
Jennifer	30 in.	7½	19
Josh	30 in.	7	19
Nick	30 in.	8	21
Mario	30 in.	8½	22
Nissa	30 in.	8	21
Erin	30 in.	7	20

Talk About

Use the charts to compare the measurements made by each child in the previous circle times. Label the top of the chart with the name or simple drawing of the item measured. How many of Jimmy's thumbs did it take to measure the door? How many of his hands? How many of Vanessa's hands did it take? How many of your hands?

Depending on the skill level of your group, you may wish to represent the totals by recording the correct number with dots as well as the numeral. Display the charts in the classroom close to the item measured.

To Extend This Circle Time

Have the children take their hand and thumb tracings home. Invite them to measure objects in their houses using their hands and their parents'.

Books to Share

Katz, Marjorie P. *Fingerprint Owls and Other Fantasies.* M. Evans and Company, Inc., 1972.
  Very simple drawings show pictures that can be made from fingerprints and a marker.

Moncure, Jane Belk. *The Touch Book.* Children's Press, 1982.
  Watercolor illustrations depict the fuzzy, cold, warm, sticky, lumpy, furry, rough, smooth, slippery and prickly things that fingers are made for touching.

O'Neill, Mary. *Fingers Are Always Bringing Me News.* Doubleday and Company, Inc., 1969.
  A collection of 14 poems about all kinds of people and the unique things their fingers can do and know.

Pluckrose, Henry. *Length.* Franklin Watts, 1988.
  Imaginative photographs and simple text introduce basics of measuring height and length by many different methods.

Tapes and CDs

Beall, Pamela Conn, and Susan Hagen Nipp. "Where Is Thumbkin?" from *Wee Sing.* Price Stern Sloan, 1977.

McGrath, Bob. "Where Is Thumbkin?" from *Sing Along with Bob, Vol. 1.* Kids' Records, 1984.

Monet, Lisa. "Where Is Thumbkin?" from *Circle Time: Songs and Rhymes for the Very Young.* Monet Productions, 1986.

Sharon, Lois and Bram. "Where Is Thumbkin?" from *In the Schoolyard.* Elephant Records, 1980.

How Tall Are We?

Name	Hands	Thumbs